T0343533

# These Strange Bodies

Court Ludwick

Copyright © 2024 Court Ludwick

All rights reserved. No part of this publication may be reproduced, distributed, or transmitted in any form or by any means, including photocopying, recording, or other electronic or mechanical methods, without the prior written permission of the publisher, except in the case of brief quotations embodied in critical reviews and certain other noncommercial uses permitted by copyright law. For permission requests, write to the publisher at the address below.

ELJ Editions, Ltd. is committed to publishing works of quality and integrity. In that spirit, we are proud to offer this collection to our readers. This is a work of creative nonfiction. Names, characters, places, and incidents either are the product of the author's imagination or are used fictitiously, and any resemblance to actual persons, living or dead, business establishments, events, or locales is entirely coincidental.

ISBN: 978-1-942004-75-2

Library of Congress Control Number: 2024945000

Cover Design: Court Ludwick

ELJ Editions, Ltd.
P.O. Box 815
Washingtonville, NY 10992

www.elj-editions.com

# Praise for These Strange Bodies

"*These Strange Bodies*, by Court Ludwick, is an incantatory and haunting collection of hybrid pieces—seamlessly moving in the liminal diastema of lyric essay and prose poem—that enact a series of powerful meditations on (dis)embodiment. Part memoir, part body horror, part catalogue of the mysteries and vulnerabilities of human physiognomy, these are pieces that unflinchingly transgress the boundary crossings and trespasses between inside and outside. Here, memories are poltergeists that linger and disrupt sinew, tissue, brain, blood, and bone. Frequently gutting, exceptionally lyrical, and relentlessly inventive, this is a riveting, skilled, and visceral debut."

—Lee Ann Roripaugh, author of *Tsunami vs. the Fukushima 50*

"With this powerful collection, Court Ludwick has pulled up a chair and taken her rightful place in our hearts and literary landscape. This debut is populated by flawlessly written essays, poems, and experimental pieces, each adorned with such clear purpose that strike at the heart, while offering us a new way of examining themes of womanhood, love, family, community, and more. I am in absolute awe of Ludwick's brilliance."

—Ukamaka Olisakwe, author of *Ogadinma*

"*These Strange Bodies* is an ethereal work that unbraids the trauma narrative through formal experimentation and fragmentation. Ludwick's journey is both kinetic and electric, slipknotting readers through painful and revelatory self-discovery, into the liminal space between sleeping and coming to. With her lyricism and poet's cadence, Ludwick reveals how assault, arson, scalpels, and other bodily and societal threats forced her into divided perspective calisthenics where she must simultaneously exist outside of the body while remaining trapped inside the silo of the self. *These Strange Bodies* is a memorable, visceral memoir. Readers will feel less alone after reading it."

—Tara Stillions Whitehead, author of *They More Than Burned*

*To Whitney*

# Contents

# The Fourth Humor Is Melancholia

**A** stranger comes over and tells me I'm hot and says they like how they can feel my ribcage through the skin and that makes me warm inside until they leave and I lie on the tile floor and I become cold again and I touch the points sticking out from my strange flesh and I touch the body that doesn't feel like it's mine. In the end, someone's protrusions become see-through under too much blue light. You shrink into yourself, into bones that have broken but have never been set.

# Somebody

Halloween. 2018. His teeth scrape against mine. Like some sort of surgical debridement grinding away much more than damaged bone, splitting down to marrow, and my eyes are open like that.

They should be closed. But my spine is shoved up against a maple staircase and my L4 is eighteen percent curved and I'm only like eighteen percent straight and he tastes like a red pack of Camel Wides and so they're not. His tongue is clumsy, dipping into my molars. His rough hands tug on my skirt's hem. The whole time, I'm wondering if the whiskers my roommate drew on my face, last minute and in thick eyeliner, will be smudged on his nose when he pulls away. He forces his knee in-between my bare legs and I try my best not to think about how his green panty hose tickle the skin but I'm high from the bag of coke my friend filched from her older sister's medicine cabinet so I laugh in his eardrum. Louder than anyone means to. It's an awful, shrieking thing.

Leaning back, away from me, he covers his ears, all *see no evil, hear no evil.* So I lean back too, shrug my shoulders, just barely, flatten spine against cracked wood, ignore my rhomboid minor, major, I don't know, some screaming muscle, like I like it, like *okay, have it your way.* I don't say sorry because I'm not. But it's not ten seconds before he pulls me back into his chest, somehow closer than before. I taste his last five smoke breaks. In this memory, I am the type of difficult that men like.

Earlier, he walks in with some of my classmates. This is before I add a second major, back when I take fashion history classes and wear silk slip dresses to brunches where nobody eats, and so everyone is bitchy and thin. He introduces himself to the room as a friend of B's, introduces himself to me later as one of B's closest friends, *even though we used to hook up*, even though she's never mentioned him before, and he probably thinks he's casual, telling me this. Clever, when he says the gap in my smile reminds him of that one pornstar (*yeah, see, you know the one*). Smarter than me when I play dumb, when he says, *I like your diastema.* He is greeted with head nods and something like disinterest. I am in love with everyone.

It's a friend of a friend's apartment, and I am on a friend of a friend's couch. Origami swanned up against hand-me-down throw pillows. And trying not to be depressed about how all the furniture is slate gray, came with the place looks like, same color as the floor. I forget who I came with, but now there's five of us kissing shoulders. I think we're all trying not to pill like the upholstery. I know for a fact that we're doing a bad job at doing damage, at weighing down the cheap foam.

For the past half hour, B has been playing musical chairs by herself. We're the chairs. The fake nail on her middle finger that she keeps refilling and shoving in our noses is the music. Someone brings up Kant. We throw popcorn at his head and skip him next round. "What?" he asks like we all should want to talk about categorical imperatives. I throw a buttery kernel at his head, and it sticks to the dimple in his cheek for longer than you'd expect.

I don't remember the first time I try a stimulant and like it better than the Gabapentin and Effexor my psychiatrist prescribes me for panic attacks. I forget when

I realize the stimulants quiet my brain instead of catalyzing a manic rush my friends describe. I don't think I ever had an addictive personality before, then during, then after. The Adderall I slip underneath my tongue even now still quiets my mind, lets me breathe, even if the effects are lessened, so maybe I'm just trying to get away from my noise.

I don't remember what time he gets to the party either because. I don't look twice when he walks through the front door, all fraternity basement and gel spiked hair and. I don't notice him staring at me until B knocks her knees into mine but. I don't get it until she loses an elbow in my ribs like ow! Then—oh. My fingers are in my mouth, I'm rubbing the stuff on my gums, when he sits down on the sagging couch arm, quickly and too close.

And then he says that line, the one about my smile, that anyone could've seen coming. And then my friends are all raised eyebrows and waiting smirks, knowing I'm about to shoot him down, maybe too harsh, like they've seen me do to guys like him before. And I just sit there. Fingers in mouth. One knee touching his. One knee touching B's. Looking up and imagining what I can say that will make him turn red and burning and embarrassed and gone.

I know everyone wants me to say something mean, say something funny, say something they expect, *say anything jesus christ!* (Kernel Dimple's eyes are screaming this), but I only laugh and motion for the boy to come closer. I look around. I know nothing bad can happen here. I grab B's finger and yank her arm across my chest and shove whatever's left up his nose so hard he bleeds.

After, he breathes like I did, waking up from that one surgery, that one time. Gasping but grateful. Now, I count to ten in my head, but there is no anesthesiologist telling me to, and I don't even make it to three before I feel his knee dig into my calf, tendon, bone, again. In my most seductive voice, I ask: "So you like Kant or what?"

B rolls her eyes at me. Everyone else goes back to the blow.

I tease him.

"Where, exactly, did you find those sexy green tights?" I whisper in his ear how Peter Pan used to be my favorite, and he teases me back, makes fun of the cat ears I scored at the 99 cent shop a block up from my apartment.

"Better than being a—what are you again?—a stripper cat."

"Sex kitten?" I scrunch up my nose, try to make the whiskers move.

"Hot."

He isn't my usual type. I like smart girls who wear ripped fishnets and apply too much blush on the apples of their cheeks, and tall boys who don't own boat shoes and are only vaguely reminiscent of anthropomorphized owls, and humans who know what I'm talking about when I talk about bad mothers and black hole singularities and the absurdity of time and the golden era of professional basketball and why stargazing is an inherently depressing act. Basically, I like people who understand why I look up at the stars anyway, people who will debate me about absolute truths for three hours on a phone call even if they agree &whatnot. Basically, this boy isn't my type at all.

But he tells me he's transferring into our school's graphic design program, tells me he's moving into the vacant bedroom upstairs, tells me he's *twenty-two right at the edge of twenty-three*, tells me he can buy me and my friends beer whenever, tells me to *stay put while I run to the kitchen,* tells me he's going to pour me a beer right now. *Stay put.* He says he likes one of the same shows I like, so I go with it. In truth, I think talking to him just reminds me of looking at stars.

An hour before I taste blood, B pulls me aside. Her nails smell like the kind of dish soap they wash baby ducks with. Her nails leave tiny crescent moons in my arm when she asks, "What are you doing?"
"What do you mean?"
"You don't like him."
"I do"
"You don't."
"I might."
"You don't."
"I *could.*"
"Jesus, fine. How are you getting home?"
I knock on her head. "Hello? I live across the street." And I can't tell if her eyes narrow or widen or float in outer space or remain asleep inside her skull. "And I promise I'll be fine." I think to myself: I shall paint her later. And I can't tell if she looks convinced or what.

So here we are on the staircase. Here is his tongue, stuck in my ear. See the boy. See him swirl his floppy tongue around&around. He bites my upper lip. God, he tastes like ash. But no, that's only the kind of wood the staircase is made of. No, that's not right. No, see, now I am the thing felled then cut then fashioned out of maple.
He's oblivious to my ticklish thighs. And. God. He tastes stale. Tastes off. Tastes funky. You can do this, though. It's simple: one must eat around the mold.

Now see the boy's mouth. Now see his tongue turn soft then hard then soft again against mine. See a meat cleaver on cutting board, all gristle, all bloody like that. See his fat, callused thumbs leave ugly pink marks on my exposed midriff. See the boy bite the girl's lip, yet again. The whole time, my eyes don't close once. And see front tooth scrape against cheekbone. See the girl and the boy making out? Right there on the staircase? Do you see the boy and the girl? See the lovers on ash, no maple, no walnut, no but who knows, maybe the boy and the girl, see, maybe they are in love.

I taste iron. But maybe it's a good thing—I'm anemic and forget to take the gummies that taste like metal most days. Also: I am almost positive that B's eyeballs were still in her head. So, there's another good thing—if we're counting. But who's counting? And hey, where did she go? Okay, so maybe her eyes were in her head, but then again, maybe not. Maybe she scraped them out with the inside of her coked-up crescent-moon fingernails. Hey, where are her warm, brown eyes?

Hard to tell when there's too many people / faces / points on a line / Real Numbers in-between Point X and Point Y. There are too many pixels, just like those stars you see in the black behind your eyes.

Fuck I hope she has her eyes because I can't see anything plus how long have I been in the dark? and why can I see *his* eyes though? as I feel his chest muscles through the flimsy polyester? some dollar store costume? and then I feel his eyes on me and then he brushes a strand of hair from my face and maybe that's the one thing I can't feel in this moment, my face, and then he slaps my jaw like a broken promise and after he asks if I want to go to Mars and never come back and then I apologize because I misremember that part sometimes.

I gasp, and he thinks I'm gasping for him. His eyes are so incredibly cold. The kind of cold you feel when you first run into the ocean, when salt dries out your tongue, when the hairs on your arm stand up straight and you go underneath for a second thinking nothing will change but so quick your eyes are watery red the color of roses and you're laughing. Full bellied laughing because it's cold all right but it's also beautiful also dangerous also you never knew oceans felt this cold, felt like this. A shock. It's a gasp. Maybe, even, a grateful one. You run into the ocean. Then he gasps, yet again. You clutch at his throat, gasping, I gasp for more air. I think I do, you think you gasp for more air.

My lip is numb. His hands move to my chin.

"Are you bleeding?"
    "Am I?" I feign surprise.
    "You are," he says, pulling my face close. In my hand: his plastic cup.
    "I couldn't tell." I pause. "It doesn't hurt."
    "Does that mean you like it rough?"
    "I just couldn't tell."

I start to turn away, but he bends my arm back like I did to B. Now see the boy peer into the girl's near-empty cup. "You need another." It's not a question. "What's your poison?" I want to laugh at how he speaks in bad movie lines.
    I flirt. "Surprise me."
And he leaves and I back up and the maple is hard again

and what is that sweetness I taste? on the tip of my tongue? and I dig thumbs into eye sockets. See stars. See those / my / shaking legs? I close your eyes for a second. Because it's simple: one must simply figure out their location on the demarcated line. See. I was supposed to memorize the names of all the constellations in the sky once. In this moment, I panic when I realize I don't know any. Later, I panic when I realize all the stars are dead. My eyes close and then the music stops. The spinning stops. The pixels, the people, the boy with the cold eyes, everything is *this* (put your thumb and index finger millimeters away but not quite together) *close* to falling off my very neat and very tidy line. And so I pull it all up like a rubber stopper on a linked silver chain. When nothing gives, I dive underwater.

And he leaves and the maple is hard again and I panic and he returns. "Hey, tired already? Hey, what gives?" I black out on the staircase.

I drive home. Today is tomorrow. The drive is exactly one hour and thirty-four minutes. Maybe a little shorter if traffic doesn't stall. Maybe a little longer if I slow down and look out the window and try to make sense of the pixelated mess.

He pulls me to my feet. "You okay?" His question—loud in my ears.

"No."

"Are you sure?"

"No."

I tell him. I tell him no.

"Okay. Good. Glad you're feeling fine." He thrusts a new plastic cup into my hands, and I take a small sip, and he grins like a bear with honey, and brown liquid sloshes around, &around.

& sometimes, when I'm looking up at the sky, I forget what the body is made of.

"And another drink?"
And another.
"Sure."
And another.
"Yes please."
And another.
"I don't feel okay."
And another.
"Hey."
And another.
"Hey, what's your name?"
&another.

"Hey, will you dance with me?" I ask. I look up at him with zero and one thousand expectations.

He takes too long to say yes so I ask him again. "Dance with me?" But this time it's not a question. I knock on his head—hello!—because now it's my turn to speak in bad movie lines.

I grab his hand and spin him around like I want to. "Isn't the guy supposed to do that?" he asks like of course he would. He laughs, pulls away and stops dancing and looks down at me, and laughs, like of course he would.

See, the boy is full bellied laughing. Just like oceans. Just like his eyes. Blue and cool so cool I catch myself frozen, but shivering, staring into them. See. They were so different from his hands. Thick-callused and dirty-nailed and angry around my waist and *warm*. I remember that. So warm, they are almost hot.

I stumble and have to grab ahold of his hands to catch myself. I giggle like a pet you want to yell at. I blow air out of my mouth because my nose is bleeding but no one ever tells me these things. Plus it's easier than you'd think it'd be—forgetting how breathing is supposed to feel.

I tug on those hands. I hyperfocus on his hands. I pull him close so I can whisper in his ear. I speak loudly and drunk.

"You're Peter Pan."

It takes him too many seconds to respond. As though he is confused. As though the words I say make zero and one thousand sense. "Am I? A lost boy or what?"

"Maybe," I don't know.

"Maybe you are too."

"I have a problem."

"What's that?" I can't tell if he's still laughing.

"I don't really like Peter Pan that much anymore." I tip my cup back until his face disappears.

He studies me like that. For the first time all night, he looks pensive. As though he is deciding something. He says this next part quietly, just quiet enough so no one else might hear, like of course he would. "You're really something."

In return, I ask him: "Are you?"

# Loose Tooth

The first time a piece of you becomes movable, you don't realize until it's too late. First time your body commits an act of betrayal, and you barely notice the slight give, but fixation doesn't take long and soon enough the enamel wears down from your obsessive tongue. Of course parents say take those dirty fingers out of your mouth. So of course you find a thin string instead. Loop it twice around their bedroom door handle out of spite then knot it good then doublecheck the bow wrapped around your lateral incisor and then slam it shut, make the drywall shake. Wet string falls pathetically to the floor. You become even more consumed. Bus ride home—you miss your stop. Favorite movie—rewind four times but you still don't quite catch that one line because you're the only thing playing on the television screen: knees to chest, esophagus exposed, hyoid bone dangerously close to being seen, and you feel wind on all your ridges. Look at your face in the gray. You remain transfixed on your tooth's give. The slack. How you have become unrooted. You are reminiscent of a broken hinge. Milk bone rattling in your milk skull, a cage more shakable than you once thought. Unsecure. Unsteady. You dream of teeth. One day you wake up from a good tooth dream. First thing you do is flick your tongue up to trace those sweet grooves but you feel only gummy flesh. Check the sheets—crimson stains—and there you are. There is a release not so sweet as you once imagined. Untethered. Now unfastened. But there's a certain freedom in flushing part of your body down the toilet and pretending your mother is mad, you mean crazy, when she asks where your front tooth has up and gone. In secret, you touch the hole it left. That emptiness tastes good, like metal and memory.

# If I Was a Psychic On a Blue Velvet Couch

At the end of summer, your mother will cheat on your father. You will not know if she has cheated before. You will not know if she has cheated with other men, in other places, when your father was living in a submarine or on a ship, or if there is more to the story. You will not know many things, but you will listen as your father and sister tell you this over the phone. When they hang up, you will skip the workshop you have later in the day with the middle-aged professor you have a crush on, and you will finish off the six-pack of Blue Moon you'd been saving for the weekend, and you will sleep for two days straight after.

But, before you do any of this, you will keep listening, confused when they keep talking. You will wonder what more there is to say. You will cuss under your breath, wonder why they had to say anything at all. And you will be even more confused when they tell you that your mother has been arrested for what the newspapers will later call "terroristic threat of family/household," what your boyfriend's family will call bad parenting, what your friends, for fear of upsetting you, will not call anything.

You will think your father is joking when he tells you that your mother tried to burn the house down with your sister and her fiancé inside of it, after they found out she was cheating on him. And, before you can stop yourself, you will laugh out loud, because you can't really do anything else.

You will think the entire phone call insane. You will imagine the red brick house on the corner of the street up in flames. You will imagine your old bedroom, still there like a memory, a half-hearted preservation of a former you, bad shrine, *gone*, because of your kerosene mother. You will laugh, until you realize no one else is and you probably shouldn't be either.

At this point, your sister's voice will stall, her eyes probably full of tears, and you will have a panic attack. This one won't last long and your breathing will slow and you will pinch the insides of your thighs as your sister tells you exactly what happened, tells you how she had no other choice but to call the police and have your mother arrested. Later, she will also tell you that she begged the cops to let your mother go, to call a psychiatrist, to call someone who might actually help, because something similar has happened before.

And you will have so many questions. You will still not know so many things. But for the very first time, you will not feel like a child left in the dark or talking to trees.

After not enough time has passed for you to process it all, your sister will say goodbye. You will ask your father if he's okay, and then listen to him lie yes. After they hang up, you will have another panic attack, a longer one this time. And, after that, you will think back to your childhood, to the fights you had with your mother once you started to grow up. You will think about the weeks when she was gone, and about the weeks when she wasn't—but was. You will remember the times when her face twisted up and her voice became guttural, inhuman, not the mother you knew. You will think back to all of this, and you will stop laughing. You will think back and know that this was coming for a long time, probably. You will skip class and get drunk and sleep for two days straight after.

In a month or so, you will visit home for the first time

in a long time. Your sister will be visiting too, and you will see her blonde hair, now dyed a dark brown, a color closer to yours, and you will think to yourself how much she looks like your mother. You will think how much the both of you have started to. You will run up to her and hug her tight. And you will put on terrible movies you both hate but love to watch together.

The night will come slow, and you will talk to your older sister about everything, but you will not talk about how your mother is gone, not yet. You will not talk about the strange empty hole you feel somewhere between your uvula and stomach, and you will not ask her if she feels that same emptiness too. You will not ask her about that day, or even how it feels being back in the house where you both grew up but where only she was when it happened. What you *will* ask is if she wants to look for *it* online. And, because you are sisters, she will not cry *vague referent!* She will know exactly what *it* you are asking about, and she will nod her head, *yes*. You both will have been waiting to do this. You both will have been waiting for the other to start.

Once you find your mother's mugshot, you will wish that you hadn't. Your sister will gasp at your mother's face, blank and pale and strange without color. And you will echo her, you have always echoed her, and you will cover your mouth with your hands as though that will help stop the painful sounds you make from coming out, as you take in her thin eyebrows, their angry slant. You will visibly cringe, your face will shimmy into a shade closer to green, when you see her eyes, eyes that you would have sworn were hazel, an in-between, but will, in that moment, look inconsolably gray.

Your father will walk into the room, ask the two of you what you want for dinner, and your sister will shut the laptop fast. You will cross your fingers and pray under your breath that he does not see, but he will. He will see his wife's face on the screen, even as it remains closed, and he will cough once, and his cough will be the kind of cough that someone makes not when they're trying to clear their throat but when they're trying to keep their guts from spilling out onto the floor, and then he will walk out of the room without saying a word. It will be your sister's turn to laugh then, and your turn to hold yourself, and her bleeding parts too, in.

You will take her hand. And she will laugh. And only you will know that she isn't really laughing.

Texas will become cold, colder than it has ever been, colder than you ever remember it becoming, and, in December, you will graduate with two degrees because you didn't know how to pick just one. You will walk across the stage when the announcer gets to the *L's,* and your family and friends will yell obnoxiously loud as you try not to blush / stumble / burn / crumple into yourself. After the ceremony, your mother will find you in the crowd, come up to you, and hand you a bouquet of sunflowers. You will not say anything as you take your favorite flowers from her hands, and she will look sad as she walks to her car alone.

When you take pictures with your grandparents, you will look a little sad too. But then you will jump in the river that everyone jumps in after graduating, and you will forget about feeling sad. You will jump only after your best friends tell you that you have to and that you'll regret it if you don't. You will jump because you'll see their smug faces and know they're right. The dress you bought will end up soaking and only a little see-through, and the two hours you spent on your hair and makeup will have been for nothing. You will see the video of you jumping in the river after, and you will not care.

After a stranger helps you climb out of the river, your best friends from back home and your boyfriend, C, will hand you the wilted roses they got from a booth outside the university arena. The roses will sit in a vase until they turn black and fall to pieces. You will keep the sunflowers your mother gave you for one day. And, when you give them to your roommate's girlfriend the next morning, you will be jealous of her gratefulness, of the joy clearly evident on her pretty, button-nosed face.

Texas will become even colder, and you will become more or less okay. You will buy a warmer jacket. You will bundle up in scarves and a hat. It will rain in the morning, and it will snow at night, but you will buy an umbrella to keep yourself dry, and you will wear the thickest socks you own. The days will grow shorter, and you will sleep even longer.

There will be a pandemic. Right before the pandemic happens, you will visit New Orleans with a few friends from high school. You will drive. Or, more accurately, your closest friend from high school will drive eight hours across state border lines while you sleep in her car's passenger seat with a thin blanket pulled over your head because a thin blanket pulled over your head will be the closest thing to a sensory deprivation chamber that you'll have. And she will be secretly happy you only drive the one time, the one hour, on the last night when everyone else is drunk, because she knows how bad you really are at driving.

It will be cold in New Orleans too, but you will borrow her skirt and wear it out at night anyway. You will put your hair in pigtails, and your other friend—the one who slept in the *backseat* with a blanket pulled over *her* head—will paint glitter over your face, over your arms, over your goosebump legs. If there is a part of your body that is visible, she will paint glitter over it. If there are parts of your body that are not-so-visible, she will paint glitter over these bits too. In the end, everyone will be glad she does this because you are the one friend who will flash the college-aged guys with plastic beads they probably would have thrown to you anyway, and the white-haired men with digital cameras who you will only notice after your shirt is already pulled up around your neck. You will laugh, not quite drunk, as they shout at your naked chest.

On the first night there, your friend—your backseat friend, not your driving friend—will want to stop on a dimly lit street corner in front of two greasy fold-up chairs and one white plastic table to have her palm read. Your other friend—the driving friend—will look uneasy, and then she will tell you both how *these people are scammers*, with tricks fake as her nails. After a few minutes, the three of you will decide to cough up twenty bucks each anyway.

Somehow, you will end up first in line, looking more nervous than anyone should, and shuffling your feet around in front of an aging woman—a self-proclaimed psychic—who will have more purple hair than gray, and a gold tooth where her left canine would have been. She will call you *honey* and tell you to sit down in a drawl much too hushed for a woman with a stolen shopping cart filled with plastic crystals and hopefully plastic skulls. And you will listen, before asking her how this all works, as if you are the type of person who would believe any answers she might give anyway.

She will take the two folded bills from your left hand and grab ahold of your right. When your eyes meet hers, she will say, "Like this."

Without even looking at the lines and scars and freckles on your palm, her eyes will close. Her grip on you will tighten. Your friends will still be behind you, now laughing at her banana yellow eyeshadow, but you will be the one her fingernails dig into. You will not laugh when you hear their jokes because you will see the same sad orange lipstick, but also the quiver of her top lip, the flutter underneath her closed lids, and instead start to think, what if this is real?

A few seconds will pass before she says anything. And when she does speak, you will wish you would've just laughed and made fun of her too. You will be silent, still, as she tells you that your mother is sadder right now than you ever will be in your entire life, that your sister has been stressed to the point of literal collapse, that an important piece of your father is close to breaking, that you are needed back home. Your friends will go quiet then, and you will pretend not to have heard whatever bullshit the batshit psychic has said. You will move your hand away, too fast and almost rude.

Unbothered, she will wave you off, wave for the next person in line, wave for your friend to come forward, and you will step aside. You will fake listen, fake laugh, fake a forced smile, at her happy predictions. You will rub your palm until the crescent-shaped marks from her hard nails turn pink and then white and then gone.

There will be a pandemic, and time will feel weird, and you

will spend your days like you used to, and you will be sleeping once again in your childhood bedroom, but the problem you will inevitably find yourself having will not be with time exactly but with the erosion that comes with it. The shape of your torso will not be quite so deep an indentation in your old mattress. The shape you will have become will not move so effortlessly within walls that were constructed some time ago. And, sooner or later, you will realize that houses do not erode at the same rate that bodies, people, you, do.

✕

Your twenty-second birthday will pass, and you will get ready to move to a new city for more school. A few days before you and your father make the seven-hour-long drive west, your mother will call. You will hit accept, because you will feel bad about all the other times when you hit decline. And then you will answer, and then you will say hello like you are really saying *leave me alone*, and then, in a voice both hopeful and strained, your mother will ask her youngest daughter if she might, just maybe, be able, even if she isn't even welcome, to stop by.

When she walks through the door without knocking first, your throat will feel like it is closing. Your mouth will feel dehydrated, unnaturally dry. You will think for a second, *am I in need of emergency intubation?* and your words will feel clumsy and rushed and not wholly yours as your brain tells your tongue to start moving, as you open your mouth and force yourself to say hello. Her smile will look awkward too, not quite right, not quite as you remember it, and you will wonder if you are hallucinating when one corner of her mouth begins to sag lower than the other. She will be wearing a tight shirt. Her midriff will be showing. Her dark pants will be loose around her waist, taut and stretched everywhere else. She will be thin, thinner than before, and she will still be pretty, she has always been pretty, she is prettiest in your memories and the old photographs you lie about keeping, but you will miss the before.

You will not remember exactly what she says—she will not stay long because your words will be cold as stars—but you will remember how she stands to leave. Slowly, as if you will forgive her. Carefully, as if you might bite. Her black eyeliner will have gone all smudged, and her maroon lipstick never did stay in the lines, and underneath her dark makeup and fake-tan skin, she will look tired. Right before she walks out the door, she will lean in for a hug and her arms will stretch out and you will try to remember if she has always looked like a puppet on a string. You will not hug her. And she will flinch. You will ignore how frail she looks when she says goodbye twice, the same way she does on the phone and in the voicemails she leaves to you, the ones you lie about deleting and not listening to.

And then you and your father will make the seven-hour-long drive west. The apartment you should have visited before signing the lease will be nice enough, but the air will be drier than you're used to. You will think maybe you should have just gone ahead with the unnecessary emergency intubation because complications are, after all, A Thing.

You will try to call C to tell him about the dry air and the funny medical joke you thought up, but he will not answer. The call will go straight to his voicemail, and you will listen to the whole thing before the beep, his boyish voice sounding different and the same, recorded back before you two even knew each other. You will wonder if he listens to voicemails like you do, or like you lie about doing. You will think about calling your mother before calling your sister instead.

Your father will stay just long enough to help you get settled in. He'll tell you that his back hurts, and he'll tell you to get off the phone, and he'll tell you to help him carry the coffee table up the stairs. You will stub your toe as you do. You will wish you hadn't moved at all. You will cuss, loudly.

As you cradle your toe, your father will tell you not to cuss so loud. You will tell him that it's his fault, you got it from him. And he will laugh, ignoring what you said, because he knows you're right. Your father will say that you need a new couch, and you will drive to some random furniture store together to pick one out, and you will do all this because you know he's right.

Too soon, he will leave and you will hug him goodbye and your new couch will be blue velvet. You will text him, *let me know when you get home*, and he will call seven hours later and say, *I'm home*. You will want to text your mother back. You will watch a horror movie with all the lights on instead. You will need to go to sleep early. But you will stay up late. You will think about sunflowers and want to cry. You will think about fires and then imploding stars and then you will punch the closest pillow. You will pinch the insides of your thighs and pretend you never stopped sleeping so many months ago. You will pretend that your blue velvet couch does not exist. You will pretend it is last summer, and you have a crush on your teacher, and you have a six-pack of Blue Moon in the fridge that you will not drink until the weekend.

## Locusts

Do they sing? I can't remember. Only a year since I saw them last but guess I wasn't paying attention. Someone told me once—maybe my mother, she loved talking about things she thought were evil—how they rub their wings together. Do they have wings? I don't remember their bodies in flight. I only recall their corpses. Or what I thought were corpses. How they littered the ground. Cloaking the trunk of my favorite tree. Once, I cradled one's molted exoskeleton, and there was no flesh inside. No dull buzz. Where was the high pitch scream? What a strange burden to carry: a shell of a once breathing thing. I held someone's skin once. Never my own. What a strange thing to hold onto. I miss that chorus, that used to keep me up at night. In my palm, it crumbles into nothing so fast.

# Room 1152

I am wearing a tight dress in a hot casino. It's my twenty-first birthday, and so I bet on red. All or nothing. Isn't that what they say? There are dancers in white feathers. Men in cheap suits. Nothing is ever dark here except maybe the dealer's wide smile. The roulette wheel spins. The color rushes into black. A chronic palpitation—everyone stutter-stops under the cheap neon lights—and July is hot. Our hotel room is waiting and cold. My feet are killing me and our room key is lost and I don't know any street names here and there's a rumor going around that the chapels never close but at least the heels I'm wearing make my legs look long.

Hands on my waist pull me in close, pull me in hard, pull me in harder than they mean to, I think. They are C's, and I laugh harder than *I* mean to, I think. Because I am drunk. Because I like how it feels. Because I like how it feels to be loved. The wheel slows, slows more.

My heels are wet, slippery, free when I take off my shoes. C gasps. "You're bleeding."

Deadpan, "I had no idea."

He calls me a shithead and asks if I want him to carry my shoes. "Want me to throw you over my shoulder, carry you back to our room?" His eyes are light brown, almost green in the sun, and they are so honest when he asks.

"Tempting," I say. "But let's stay here a while."

A thick-lashed bartender brings me another drink. And the hands on my waist become the hands on my shoulders. The hands on my neck. Behind me, someone shouts. *Color up.* Behind me, *Party foul!* Every so often, C leans down so I can smell his aftershave. How am I doing?

Doing okay? Do I want water? Is there anything I need?

You, I think. "No," I say out loud, even though the room spins. Because I like how it feels to be loved by him. I lean back like a trust fall. His chest catches me, and I don't think he notices how sturdy he is, the way he's just there.

"I promise I'm not thirsty," I have to tell C twice in ten minutes. I don't have to explain how the water in casinos tastes of pennies and rust. He doesn't ask.

The wheel lands on black, and my heel is still bleeding red. I lose fifty bucks, and then fifty more. Cards whisper. Dice fall. Giddy screams from the feather dancers. Catcalls from men with almost-wives. Bodies rush together, but I feel nothing on my skin.

*I feel nothing on my skin.* I look around. He's not anywhere. *Better luck next time, doll.* The woman has teased hair and an accent I can't place. *You all done, sweets?* She must be southern—different state than us though. Someone throws money down, and I feel the wheel move.

I feel the whole car move. It swerves to the right, into the other lane for a second. There are no cars behind me. Only behind and up ahead. No passengers to yell at my old memories. No drivers to scream bloody, overdramatic murder. In need of a tether, I grab the cracked steering wheel with both hands. In front of me, the highway is blue and endless. In front of me, the blue road becomes that blue night. I cuss. I don't want to remember. I cuss. I pretend I'm heading somewhere else.

And then I am ten in a different July. I know nothing of catcalls or casino water or why people wear shoes that make their feet bleed. I'm ten and barefoot, running through rain to the neighbor's house to ask if my childhood best friend can play.

There's a doorbell, but I knock on wood like I always

do. Plus knocking feels safer this way, connecting my entire fist to sturdy wood instead of poking at the lit-up button with a single finger. After a minute or so, my best friend's mother answers, like she always does. And she knows what I'm going to ask. But she lets me ask anyway, every time. I think she knows my own mother is at home, and that I don't ever have to ask *her*.

After we promise to come inside right away if we see lightning, she says yes. *But* be safe. We bob our heads up and down. And don't run so fast. We smile our serious smiles. She tells us to come inside and dry off when we get cold. She tells us to grab a hoodie, off the rack, before we go. She says be safe once more and her words hug us tight as if we didn't hear this week before last. She speaks but we are children so who knows if we listen.

A is one year younger than me and she has bangs cut too short and too often and her pleated socks match all of the time and her mother makes her wash her hands for thirty seconds when she comes in from outside. Every time? My mouth pops open. Every time. Her nod is solemn.

I am wearing one blue sock, one off-white, and both have a hole where my big toes poke through, and my mother never talks about electrocution like A's mother does now. When I say bad words, my mother sticks a bar of soap in my mouth and tells me to think about what I've done. She puts soap in your *mouth*? A's almond eyes pop open. A doesn't say bad words in front of her mother at all—and only once in front of me. Yeah, soap tastes terrible. I fail at mimicking her solemnity.

I am taller than A, but she is faster. She runs to the field behind our houses, and I try my best to keep up. The rain swallows us whole and her mother shouts at us but the screen door slams before we hear her words. The rain swallows everything. Still, we feel safe knowing she watches from the window, hands curved around her eyes, like she's blocking out the sun in order to see us better, only there aren't any harsh rays right now.

Later, as we run close to the cars on the street, I secretly hope my mother is watching us from the window too. I would never tell A this. But I look at the blinds a hundred times, even though I know they will stay drawn and closed. The only thing I see is rain. Plus my best friend all blurred. Her short bangs are wet and matted and stuck to her forehead. And of course I see her mother, waving frantically from behind their window. I see lightning, burning yellow.

I see lightning in the rearview. See rain and cuss and I know it's a bad habit but it's one of the only things my mother truly hated, noticed. I don't bother turning on the windshield wipers because they're broken but I wonder if I should stop at a gas station when the cars around me turn into blobs and the dead flies wash away. I imagine they're still alive, the flies, letting go only when their little legs and arms can't hold on any longer.

My vehicle swerves. I imagine the rain stopping soon, maybe in a few miles, black clouds cracking open to show me pale sky. My vehicle swerves again, badly this time, and I veer into another lane. I cuss, again. The car horn screaming at me tastes as bad as my mother's bar soap, maybe worse because bar soap isn't all that bad, don't tell my mother, but either way I cuss at that too. A few miles later, the sky is unchanged. Blue and black and drawn and closed.

But the sky is so pink, a stupid pink, a pink so pink I swear it isn't real, when C breaks up with me. I make a joke about how stupid it is, stupid pink sky, but he doesn't laugh. I make a joke about how stupid it is, driving nine hours to surprise someone you've loved for three years and then they don't even fake laugh at your stupid pink sky joke. I wait for him to laugh. C says I need to leave. I'm still angry he sent me to voicemail that one time. He's angry I'm on his doorstep. I realize the breakup is real then.

He says I need to find a hotel. He says long distance sucks so that's why. I nod my head and tell him I agree. That's why I drove nine hours to see you, that's why. He says he still loves me it's just that you're too much sometimes your panic attacks are too much all the time and no really you don't understand the toll they take on me do you understand the toll you take on me? He's not a bad person because he tells the truth. He's a bad person because now I think about him whenever I see a flamingo-colored sunset—that's why.

I leave. I find a hotel. Find a bottle of expensive hotel beer, *bottles* of expensive hotel beer. Then, I realize I've been in a relationship for three years and it's about time I find a someone else. In the morning, I wake up after checkout time, and my someone else has left *with* the bottles of my very expensive hotel beer. I delete my someone else's number and I call the front desk saying sorry but can you charge the card for another night and I go back to sleep until the sky goes dark. I wake up and vomit in a plastic cup. And it's night, but I check out early. It's night when I drive nine hours back. The sky is not fake-liar pink, goddamn flamingos, and there are no cars on the road.

There are no cars on the road now, as I get closer to where I've somehow ended up. The sky is still mad, raining and blue, but I decide it'll be fine if I let the colors run together for a little while. I'll be fine if I swerve into the next lane over.

I say goodbye over and over and over. In the Polaroids I rip off my apartment walls. In the drunk texts I send. In the two-in-the-morning voicemails I leave. In his defense, I am a Romantic With Issues. In my defense, he knew that before we fell in love. I say goodbye for the last time in a story, in the most melodramatic way. I email it to him, and he finds my last goodbye like that. In my defense, I am something like twenty-two plus.

"It made me sad," he tells me later.

"It was supposed to be happy."

"But are you happy? Like really?"

I don't know what he wants me to say so I lie and say I'm fine. "I'm seeing someone special, someone new." It's not the truth until way later. I hate Octobers, after.

I don't know if I hate Octobers still.

I learn about haboobs in my new city and decide I hate those too. Later, I decide that the word is okay, haboob, but West Texas is all red dirt and tangled hair and it remains decidedly hated until I start to fall in love again. In my defense, I am something like twenty-three. And so the hate seeps away, but never completely, and even now I can honestly say I hate how the sidewalks here don't get salted when it snows. In this place, you cannot run and play without slipping and stumbling and falling too.

My car windows are all fogged up, and I slide across wet road.

How easy it is.

The first after C has blonde curls. He uses a blue and white striped tie on my wrists, then binds me to his bed frame. I can't move. This doesn't feel good. He wants to be a fifth-grade teacher. Can you loosen it a bit? I think he is one now. He tells me about the children he will teach one day soon. He grabs my throat and slams me into soft pillow. You like that? I do. I don't. I don't know what I do. I drink gas station wine until I forget the color of his eyes.

The next is sweeter. She takes me to the drive-in but doesn't try to hold my hand. Black hair is longer than mine, with glasses slipping off her nose like a too-big sweater I steal from someone else. We share a bag of popcorn, her treat. She texts me after and says sorry I didn't kiss you. I don't text back for no good reason.

And the next is younger. She buys me dinner, but I kiss her first. Maybe this is why she invites me back to her place, but I have no clue why her roommate makes us sleep on the couch. We don't sleep. We barely speak. The same movie runs on a loop. I sneak out, soon as it's morning, and a few hours later she tells me to come back over—she bought donuts. We hang out until she leaves for home, leaves for the summer, leaves for good. I think she's one of my dream paralysis demons, creeping near the foot of my bed and everything, years later.

To summarize: there are red and black colors on the wheel, only I can barely tell the difference. There are hands—not his. There are ugly ties leaving angry red marks on my skin. There are cheap suit men and casino catcalls begging me to answer. There are bodies I don't know. There's my body, still doesn't feel like mine.

Unsalted, I run.

Unsalted, I fall.

In and out of these fragments, and the steering wheel turns cold like everything is. I run a red light. I am close to the place I hate. When it turns dark like this, I can barely see the highway.

I can barely see through cigar smoke. Casino air paws

at my face, my airway, like casino air tends to do. When I find him, I find him alone, near a Blackjack table, an expensive one where nobody sits. *Why did you leave me?* He asks if my feet are bleeding still. Both of us say: I don't know. Both of us reach for the other without explanation. C cashes out his chips and I hold onto his arm. Cashier smiles like she knows too much and I wish she would count the bills faster. I squeeze C's hand but not hard enough. One more drink before we head up? No, no thanks.

July is hot and our hotel room is cold. The windows are open. Curtains thrown back. Cars the size of beetles speckle the earth below and people buzz like fireflies on the strip. See their joy. Sometimes it's okay to remember the good. In my defense, I am still only twenty-five. Here, people make their drunken noise in day and in night. Then, we listen to the strange human noise they make. And, in the moment, I forget that some memories should be savored while you're in them so I open my mouth like of course I would and say: *y'know I read somewhere that if you aren't seeing fireflies in places where you used to, it's because we've made everything so inhospitable for them and they're dead, but don't quote me on that because I forget where I read it.*

C kisses me because I don't think he knows what to say. Plus the moon is full, or nearly full, and people under moons are supposed to kiss like how the poets used to talk about before poets got scared to talk about moons. Blue light in blue ribbons falls across a blue bed. And have I told you the rest of that other blue story yet? I fall across the bed. Unbutton his shirt. I wonder if I am blue too. He kisses my nose, and I think I must be.

The highway blues blur with the hotel room's. My dress falls off the bed, and I never see it again. The heat of that July burns this October. That night, I am wearing a tight dress in a hot casino. Some nights, I remember / forget / remember how it feels to be loved. I miss my exit and cuss at no one. He reaches for my hand. Kicks off his worn, scuffed shoes.

## Anatomy Class Is For Lovers

**B**ecause how can it not be when you find out the blush on your cheeks is adrenaline? When your lab partner hands you a folded note, teacher asks: did you know your stomach lining is reddening too? Once you discover the heart can sync to a song, you want to listen to someone else's playlist. Is your 150 beats per minute fast or what? A boy in front is confused—what do you mean the tongue is also a muscle—but you already know the answer. What you want to know instead is whose song will help slow you down. Daydream about mucosa and papillae and French kissing. Wonder if you could find a tether good as the frenum. Crack your knuckles, nitrogen bubbles. Snort when you realize the brain isn't fully developed until 25 because no wonder you're all messed up. Before class: bet you guys didn't know the longest fit of hiccups lasted 68 years. First bell rings. Bet *you* don't know how to get rid of them with a bitten pencil and cup of water. Are the bite marks necessary? Is the funny bone a nerve? Yes—the dust in your apartment is dead skin, and isn't it sort of lovely how you shed like that? The idea sweeps you up. Fuck, you need thicker skin. Steal it from the soles of your feet where it's thickest. Thinnest on the eyelids so maybe that's why you cry even when you're happy even when you're mad not because your sun sign is Cancer. But what's your moon sign? Lab partner's ink stains your fingers black but junk science has no place in the classroom. Teacher warns. When he turns, you whisper Pisces. On the chalkboard: the hand has 54 bones. And you want to hold all of hers. If acid in the stomach can dissolve metal, how do all those butterflies stay alive? You learn that bones are stronger than steel, pound for pound, so maybe that's what's trapping you. Is marrow sticky? Feeling stuck? They call it ribcage for a reason but can we go back to the integumentary system for a second? Teacher nods. Lab partner's shoulder touches the singing heart on your sleeve. Your stomach lining is magenta. Okay so let's review. Isn't it sorta beautiful how the skin is the largest organ and also the only one that's ever felt?

# Telephone Game

*You would look so pretty if you smiled.* You would look so pretty if you came over here and smiled. You would look so good if you came over to my house and smiled. You would look so hot if you came over to my apartment and we kissed and you smiled. You would look so hot if you came over after midnight to the apartment I share with three other middle-aged men, we're only slightly balding, we're only slightly creepy you know, and smiled. You would look so hot if you came over and maybe your friend could come over too and oh you don't know her? and I know we don't know each other but maybe we could fuck anyway and then I know you would look so pretty but only if you smiled. You would look so pretty honestly, probably, and like the hottest you've looked, maybe in the entire history of forever, if you came over and fucked me even though I'm a crazy stranger who thinks you, and all women really, should smile for me, yeah not like that though, and so what if you stopped and listened and talked, well maybe not talked, but what if you stopped and listened and did exactly what I asked you to, yeah like smile, just because I asked nicely and then not nicely and also I deserve it, well I deserve something don't I? because I didn't even yell, well not at first anyway, and why are you not stopping? and why won't you smile? and what if you did? just because I'm nice enough not to punch you square in your too-round face? and hey who's getting all worked up now? no need for theatrics! we're all thespians here, eh? and so what is this? bitch! so you're a bitch who isn't going to smile for me? and also a whore? bitch! slut! whore! I hope you die! die, you fucking ugly slut! and also, like, just maybe if I take it all back, well, like, well what if you smiled? *You would look so pretty if you smiled. So go ahead and smile for me, baby girl.*

*Can I buy you a drink?* Can I buy you a drink even though you're so pretty and so I'm assuming you have a boyfriend? Can I buy you a drink even though you're telling me you aren't into dudes like me and also, wait what the fuck, you're telling me a girl who looks like you has a girlfriend? and you're not into dudes at all now? is that it? Can I buy you a drink even though you've been rejecting my drink offer for the past ten minutes, well maybe thirty, and y'know ever since I cornered you after you left my side at the bar to go to the ladies you've been acting like a real bitch so basically I'm wondering if all this "no" talk is because you're on your period? and oh! is that why you don't want this drink because I don't mind period sex believe me! so the answer is yes now, yeah? Can I buy you a drink even though you've apparently been sober the last thirty years even though I know for a fact that's a lie because I only hit on nineteen year olds and so there's no way you're even old enough to drink in the first place, and can you clear some things up because I think you're being really fucking dumb and confusing right now? but also can I buy you a drink even though you say you won't put out? Can I buy you a drink even though you say you won't put out because I say you will? Can I buy you this drink I already bought and am thrusting into your hand because, well, I spent money on you, you ungrateful bitch? Can I buy you a drink, like the very same drink I'm currently forcing into your mouth and past your tongue and down your throat because I know you like it like that you slut! and, well, come on! don't you? Can I buy you a drink just because I saw you had long hair and I kinda wanted to pull it for half a second and sorry I think I hallucinated for a second because I imagined you shaking your head no and what? oh! so you *are* shaking your head politely no! and I think I'm going to threaten you with bodily harm now because I spent money on this drink you didn't ask for, and then more money on a second drink you begged me not to buy, and okay so like, to be fair I had already bought the drink before I even mentioned it because I figured an ugly slut like you would jump at the chance to ride such a hot dude like me, and it's really fucking weird how much better than me you think you are, don't you? and maybe that's because you're delusional, right? but hey, I like crazy, every hot girl's a little crazy! heh heh amirite? but what do you mean, you still don't want it? like what do you actually mean!? because, like, I am literally the kindest dude, sorry I mean person you nonbinary freak, who ever walked the face of this earth, and you're truthfully not even pretty and you're actually not even my type and you're honestly the ugliest fucking girl in this godforsaken bar c'mon guys let's go but you really won't take just one sip and you really won't punch my number into your phone? and whoops here it is, better drink up! even though you told me not to, and so, yeah, would you like another drink after this one? *Can I buy you a drink? It is, after all, just a drink.*

*Your skirt is pretty short.* Your skirt is pretty short and pretty slutty. Your skirt is pretty short and also way too slutty, and that makes us think you are a slut too. Your skirt is pretty short and that means you must be a slut, doesn't it? you know that's what you're saying, right baby girl? and also your skirt means you must not have said no. Your skirt is pretty short and a skirt that short and that slutty means you must not have said anything. Your skirt is pretty short so that means you must have said yes. Your skirt is pretty short and that means you one hundred percent said yes. Your skirt is pretty short and, well, you know what that means? because we think it means you teased and begged and made him, yeah, actually, you were the one who made him! Your skirt is pretty short, and we say one thing about it, yeah all the slut stuff, but also you don't care? and also you won't go home and pretend this never happened and pretend that you are lying to us right now? but we called you a slut! but we told you what everyone would think! and for Christ's sake why are you crying? because why are you still here? and why won't you go home? and, okay, so we aren't allowed to say this, so we will say it off record, so we will say you are a slut off record, so we will say you begged for it off the record just this one time okay? but oh! you want this on the record? And you don't want to pretend this never happened? and, wait, what do you mean, you don't want to pretend this never happened! slut! *Your skirt is pretty short. You sure you want to report this, baby doll?*

*You might be overreacting.* You might be overreacting because you might be misremembering the night because you might be misremembering all of it because it was pretty late because he was asking nicely at first because he does have pretty blue eyes yeah? because you were drinking before then right? because you were high as fuck weren't you? because you were wearing a skirt that was pretty short because that means slutty because all this is according to you so don't get mad at us and also let the record show that when you were buying this skirt in the store you said and I quote *tell me the truth, I kinda look like a slut in the best way, don't I?* because you do flirt quite a lot because you do like to do things that hurt you sometimes because you are pretty fucked up from all the things that have happened before because you might be misremembering all those nights too and you might be overreacting so come on accept it. *You might be overreacting. (But you know you're not.)*

# Panic Disorder

## Abstract

I daydream about amygdalotomies more than I should. I research last-ditch psychosurgery options when I probably just need to breathe or something. I use star-wishes on delusional meet-cutes: cluster of cells, sweet limbic structure, gray matter I want you to meet mechanical destruction. Or maybe an injection of oils and waxes and alcohols would be better. Death by radiofrequency. Let's get one thing straight: I am not a doctor. Most nights, I count hertz instead of sheep.

## I. Introduction

The amygdala is almond-sized, so I suppose the shape of fear is an almond. My question is this: are we allowed to rip it out, straight from the temporal lobe? I'm going to go out on a limb and say most humans are terrified—the *thing* doesn't matter—but I don't mind terror. I mind how the body feels terror, how my body responds to emotion. The act of fear is rooted in panic. And I don't know if my premise is right. (It's not.) But *can I remove my own amygdala?* Anyway, some governmental agency puts my name on a watchlist because this is what I type in the search bar and ask my sister when we talk on the phone.

The internet talks of aggressive patients who become docile with no side effects afterward. The internet says certain epileptic patients have benefitted from the procedure with limited adverse results. I want to know how they're defining side effects. I want to know who determines what constitutes an adverse result. I want to know most about off-label use.

Gabapentinoids treat seizures and fibromyalgia, but my psychiatrist says my panic disorder is treatment-resistant and fills out a prescription for 150 capsules of those suckers. They work, so all I want to know is if ripping the almond out is an option. My psychiatrist, bless Dr. Z, asks if I'm joking. I say yes. She asks if I've been experiencing intrusive thoughts again. I look around my apartment, mostly calm, and I see no pliers, only a pair of clean, kitchen scissors. A single dinner knife. I have exactly five-eighths left in an extra-large bottle of hand sanitizer. In a pinch, a half-full decanter of forty proof liquor. I'm only joking, I tell my sister. She's doing a psych rotation. I ask her if I should be focusing on the hippocampus instead. She shakes her head and her blonde hair gets in her eyes and the tips of her fingers tremble for only a moment—this is how I imagine it when I ask her these things over the phone, as I hear only sharp intake of breath—and she says she has a patient that reminds her of me. Okay, let me back up.

II. Case Presentation

It feels like this. You're sitting in the backseat of a car, looking out the window to the highway, watching the water droplets run together until your vision becomes unfocused, seatbelt too high so it's rubbing your shoulder raw, and you pause at that discomfort, but then you brush it off, plus you register how you feel fine, but you also know you're driving out of the lightning storm's eye right back into something bad, but you're also not the one driving so who cares if your right foot twitches for the breaks, and then you catch your reflection in the window, and you notice something off, only you can't tell what, only the rain is making the image blurry, only your brain translates *something off* to *something terribly wrong*, and even though you know you'll be okay eventually because lightning doesn't really kill anyone does it? plus you've seen your face look a little off before right? or have you? you also know something is on the other side of the eye-of-the-storm's quiet, and so the *I'm fine* falling out of your mouth magics itself into a lie even if it was the truth when your brain first told your mouth to open, plus you remember that lightning kills something like twenty people every year, and that's just in your country alone, and that's not even taking into account how death by lightning wouldn't even be the worst thing that could happen because what's worse is the neurological damage you'd have to live with for the rest of your life after the fact, and none of this even considers, not for a single slice of time, how the language you use also, always, uses phrases like truth and fact, as though you believe in them, as though you don't hickey into a bruise once you notice how ingrained everything is, and all this as your tongue swells into a shape you inevitably fail to attach words to. & then breathe breathe (you have to think this part) numb hands well thassokay breathe breathe blood pressure rises like the rest of you and you know there was something about grounding and the five senses and naming a thing by its color that you were supposed to hold in your brain but you question this premise like all the rest because holy fuck shut up and breathe before black-out vision around your peripherals plus the adrenaline spike and then / now cortisol breathe until something happens like a dilation of the pupils and breathe breathe! breathing! but you forget to breathe like you always do and so when you finally feel like you can again you suck in air like you have none and now you're breathing in like you never did.

## III. Discussion

I've heard people call it an out-of-body experience. And I think that's a nice image. I think it's so nice, I wish I could buy it and hang it up on a wall. But I don't know if I feel outside of my body so much as I feel like I've forgotten where I left my coat so now I'm putting on a stranger's jacket and the fabric doesn't smell like you and now I'm thinking about why I switched perspective in the middle of a sentence and does this mean I'm going to die?

They say it's a normal physiological fear response to danger—the only problem is you're not in any danger, and also you could think of an infinite number of problems if you really wanted to, and also you'll think about all of them anyway, even though you don't really want to. They say colors look different—but you always suspected this, and years before / after your diagnosis, you get into an argument about the subjectivity of color perception. They say to ground yourself—and at first you think: this, if anything ever really can be, is true. Later, you discover that even grounding doesn't prevent a lightning strike.

And turns out there is at least one side effect of amygdala removal: *deficits in specific areas of memory have been noted pertaining to recognition and emotional interpretation of facial stimuli.* I'll take it, I say. I'm joking, I lie. My psychiatrist raises her eyebrows. I find myself in a shape that no one ever pulled up on the overhead projector and pointed to with a ruler in school. Can I at least make a joke about no longer having to look my memories in the face? At least my sister laughs.

Gray. The dashboard. Off-white. My discolored shoes. Counting colors helps, they—who is they?—say. You look up at the ceiling no matter where you're at when your hands start to go numb and you count the holes in the slats because counting colors when colors are all fucked up, patterned breathing, nothing works when you think your chest, *you*, are caving in.

# Multiple Choice Practice Question

**W**hich of the following best defines the phrase "out of body?" Please circle the correct answer.

A)   Strange (adj.) from late 13c., *straunge*, "from elsewhere, not belonging to the place where found." From Old French *estrange*, "foreign, alien, unusual, unfamiliar, curious, distant, inhospitable, estranged, separated." From Latin *extraneus*, "external, from without."

B)   A detachment. A split. A (reverse) possession (of sorts).

C)   Once, I dreamt I was a ghost, haunting rather than haunted.

D)   What if *elsewhere* is *right here?* What if *place* is *body* and *body* is *mine? What if *foreign* is not *alien* is not *unusual* is not *unfamiliar?* What *is* curious is that *distant* is *close.* Does this make the flesh *inhospitable? Estranged,* I admit to feeling *separated.* What if I told you feeling *external* is *from within?*

E)   This is not a ghost story. This is a story about ghosts. & I am the lamp-throwing poltergeist.

# The Grove

**A** stranger sleeps in my bed. It doesn't matter what they look like. I should be asleep in my bed. It doesn't matter that the sheets have been thrown off, kissed and cast aside. Damp pillows and barren mattresses can still be slept on. I know this, even if I can't sleep on them right now. Instead, I stand in the doorway. I steal a cigarette from the stranger's coat pocket. Wool scratches my knuckles, and I stare at their face, handsome, beautiful even as I sober up and cough on my own sour tongue.

This stranger is older than me. A good dancer. A good kisser. Nice talker. Earlier, we talked for hours. After ordering orange beer for me, a cherry vodka sour for them, they asked me where I would go right now if I could go anywhere in the world. And it was a good question, one I'd used to fill silences on first dates before, but I didn't want to tell them the truth. I didn't want to lie either, so I flipped it around.

"Why can't I?" I asked, sucking the orange rind that came floating in my glass. "Go anywhere, I mean."

I had to stifle a laugh when their eyebrows drew close, together. "What are you talking about?"

"You said *if.* *If* I could go anywhere in the world right now." I leaned back as far as I could without falling off the barstool. "Who says I can't?"

"You just told me you teach on Fridays."

"So?"

"So it's Thursday."

"And?"

"And you can't cancel class just because you feel like it. And you can't find a flight—" They snapped their fingers. "Just like that. And you can't—"

"I—we—can do whatever we want. *If* we want to." I nudged their shoulder with mine. "Where would *you* go right now?"

"Japan?"

"Cool, let's book a flight."

"You're ridiculous."

"Roundtrip or one-way?"

"And you still haven't answered."

"Neither have you."

"Where would you go?" A pause. "If you could snap your fingers—"

"I can't snap."

"*If* you could snap your fingers and go right now."

✕

I am in the grove behind my grandparent's house. I'm a child here, and my ears stick out. My limbs grow long. My limbs grow skinny. My limbs grow embarrassed. Running without stopping to catch a breath is easy. When I talk, the trees talk back.

And I climb over their gnarled arms—not dead, uplifted root. I leap over an entire ocean—not the small creek bed that always dries up in July. I eat grapes before they ripen. I bite into berries that I think might turn my skin green or lemon yellow. Everything without a name is dangerous. The sky is a kaleidoscope, full of in-between colors that I have no names for.

✕

I can't remember the last time I was there, only that it was the last time, and that too much time has gone by since. I can't remember an exact age, a date, whether it was winter or if the small stream running through the grove really *was* dried up. I could write a hundred pages about the jokes I told to the trees though, their shocked 'O' mouths, but don't worry I won't. Just saying, memory is funny like that.

I steal a second cigarette. I don't even smoke. I listen to my stranger's uneven breathing, their strange sleep sounds. I count to one hundred and hope a storm comes. Lightning and clouded constellations. I count to two hundred and hope my stranger wakes up. They need to vomit beer on my pillows, on my carpet. They need to say sorry and say sorry again and say sorry, so sorry a third time. They need to vomit, again. My stranger needs to drive home with both hands on the steering wheel and fall asleep on their roommate's couch still in clothes and call in the morning and say sorry, so sorry! really! and then hang up and then look down and then realize they left their favorite sneaker at my place and never say a thing after.

It won't matter what they won't say. They all look the same. They say the same things. They sleep in my bed when I can't. I smoke five cigarettes in less than an hour, and I don't even smoke. They make their strange sleep sounds, and I count to three hundred. I hope their toes are cold.

The first time I go into the grove by myself, I look over my shoulder after every step. I am scared the small yellow house will move or fly away. I am scared the grass stains on my denim knees will dry and crumble and stay green forever instead of changing back to blue. I am scared the almost purple grapes are poisonous. I'm scared I will bite into their flesh anyway.

Sometimes I think I shouldn't remember these things from

my childhood. So specific, these splinters. Even now, my pink haired lover turns to me after I say something, and tells me that my memory is wild, insane, like *how do you remember that?*

*Maybe I don't*, I reply. After all, I am not remembering a memory. Only a memory of a memory of a memory of one.

×

I count to four hundred and walk past my bathroom mirror. There's a photograph of me at four years old taped up beside it, and I try to be quiet as I take it down, remove it slow so the apartment's off-white wall paint won't come off too. An absolute truth? I want my $150 deposit back.

I count to five hundred, and there's the same gap tooth smile I have now, same messy hair, same freckles. A hat too big for my head drops over my left eye. My bare feet are either dirty or the ink has gone all wonky. Someone's shadowy hand is in the bottom-right corner. And the paper is faded, but the picture isn't gone yet. I can still make out the colors. My blue shirt. Smack dab in the middle of all that blue, there's a fat yellow sunflower screen-printed on. Hanging off my shoulder, there's a reusable shopping bag I used to think was a purse. There's the camera flash. Catching my scrunched nose, as I look up at midday, and whoever was taking my picture.

I count to six hundred and flip the photograph over. On the back, there's black ink. Cursive letters spell out my name. I try to make out what's next to it, but my mother's thumb has smudged the date.

×

The second time I venture into the grove, I don't look over my shoulder once. Instead, I run. Fast as I can. Not stopping to tie my undone laces. Until my grandparent's house is the size of a dime, I run. I also fall. Don't get right back up like I feel compelled to now. Let my hair tangle with the cool brown earth and rock. The scar is almost white today.

I smoke another cigarette. This one is not stolen. I do not smoke, I keep telling myself, as I blow rings into the bathroom mirror. I do not drink. I do not swallow. I do not breathe. My tongue is hardening clay, and I am a statue. I don't do any of it—things I have done to my body before. I am granite and unmoving and dust and rock. I lay still on the bathroom floor, a Greek bust of Aphrodite. My tongue feels like rotten cotton candy. I am a Roman Venus carved in marble. No matter how many times I count to one hundred, there is no big storm and I do not scream. I toss a still burning cigarette into the tub. Curl my body into fetal position and try to fall asleep on the cold tiles.

Once, when I am seven or close to it, I stay in the grove longer than I should. When the sun starts to go down, I linger. It has been a while since I was here last—weeks are the same as forever to a child—and I don't like how the calluses on my thumbs have started to give way to the soft, pink flesh underneath. Maybe I have turned into a berry.

This is part of the reason why I don't listen when my mother calls out my name. Instead, I run. Faster than is safe. I am tired of her holding on to me so tight. *For safe keeping*, she sighs when she rocks me to near-sleep and smells my hair. Another absolute truth? I do not feel all that safe with her.

That is another reason why. I climb. A great big oak.

This one has no face. Couldn't give away my secrets even if it wanted to. No mouth to speak. And I climb too high. The branches become thin up here. Do I only imagine the air becoming thin like that too?

I dream of strangers. In return, they steal my sheets. They take my pillows. They kiss my forehead. Taunt me with questions I cannot answer. They vomit in my favorite shoes. Or maybe theirs. They make me tell them the truth, and after I do, they tell me how easy it is to go back. They say it sounds like a nice little thicket. I correct them: *grove*.

They taste of plastic peppermint candy, not grandfather's peppermint bark. They call me the wrong name and I let them. They strip my mattress bare. Get mad when we don't fuck. I'm a tease, some say. But the worst ones are the sweet ones, the ones who seem to understand, strangers who suffocate me into their chest, the ones who get it but leave anyway, strangers who hold me close like I won't cry about some thicket I used to run around in tomorrow when they're long gone. And it doesn't matter whether they remember to grab both their shoes or neither or just the one.

My legs swing out underneath me. The wind is faster at night. I keep telling myself that the sky has barely turned magenta, and it's not night yet, not truly, and I am afraid for only a second. My arms are not so wiry as they were before summer and the growth spurts that summer brought. They pull me up, unfailing.

This is how I remember it anyway. Maybe I fall. Maybe I don't. Maybe it was you up there swinging, clutching at bark and branch and feeling scared you might lose yourself to the wind. Probably me though. I think I have always been afraid of losing things. Lately, I can't decide whether memory is the one way we hold onto our past selves, or the one way we lose everything.

Anyway, I need to leave this body.

I need to love this strange flesh—I let my strangers try.

And everyone knows that suns don't go away. Suns don't disappear so fast, so easy—I try to snap—or yeah, something like that.

If I squint, the small yellow house is a sun.

# Feed

*June 3, 2019. Instagram post. (Insert tongue emoji.) (@ username of the band we went to see.)*

**I** swear on my life that the music is 115 decibels, minimum. And the bodies pressing into me like erosion become blurry then nonexistent. Plus: if it walks like a duck and talks like a duck, then the duck is most likely a panic attack, so I tug on C's shirt hem and say, *I'm going to the bathroom.* He doesn't say anything out loud, but his face contorts into some kind of question I'm not sure how to answer. *I'll be quick,* I smile.

The name of the venue is The Paper Tiger (don't forget the *The*) and I don't know the band but earlier C played me a song of theirs and asked if I liked it. I said yes when I meant to say no. Less than five minutes later he asked a question out loud for once, what if we go and see them play?

At concerts, we have to stand in the back because C's too tall to do anything else. Seventy-seven inches, give or take. I first started crushing on him when I was a cheerleader on the sidelines of his basketball games. Now, I stand on my tiptoes, trying to see the keyboard player C keeps calling hot. And now I'm in the bathroom trying not to vomit and choke on it.

*(148 likes.)*

*August 27, 2021. Instagram post. "Impulsively buy a ticket to NY for the weekend, yes or no?"*

I down three Adderall tablets and one Ritalin capsule, take and post a mirror selfie, and then have a three-minute-long phone conversation with an old friend who's currently in upstate New York dealing with Family Issues. At this point, I've started taking more than my prescribed dosage because I'm trying to bypass Just Quiet and get to the noise that feels better than numb, get to the feeling that's a paradoxical kind of loud, the kind of loud that's so loud it becomes quiet.

An hour or so later, I buy a plane ticket. I meet up with the old friend. We go out, get plastered the first night, cuddle together in the hotel's king-sized bed. On the second night, he takes me to Central Park because I want to see ducks. Then we eat some pizza and do Other Tourist Things and later that night I meet a girl at a cocktail lounge who I might have fallen in love with for just the briefest of moments.

We drink. I throw up on a sidewalk. A stranger-man yells at us. A stranger-man yells at me. Stranger-man keeps yelling at me while I

vomit two hundred dollars
of cheap liquor down
stinking city gutter. I vomit
as he yells, I swear he yells
this, but who would
fucking yell this except
those anti-drug people who
came to everyone's schools
and put on bad skits:
*bulimia isn't cool anymore and
you should grow up.* I start to
cry—I mean to yell back—
until I vomit everything up
all over again.

*(171 likes.)*

*August 28, 2021. Instagram carousel. "Body ody ody." (@ the
MoMA.)*

It's an Edward Hopper
painting, and the viewer is
a voyeur, almost like you,
almost like I'm doing that
POV switch thing again,
and you're looking in at a
woman bent over in a
salmon dress.

It's a Picasso painting, in all
that late-life Cubist glory,
and I can't tell if you like
the oblong shape with its

closed eyes, refusing to look anyone in the face, or if you hate it, because either way you keep staring, because the way the elbow is positioned reminds you of the crick in my neck that even rough fingers never completely get rid of.

It's a photograph, not a painting this time, and I don't catch the artist's name, but I can tell it's a manipulated one, of a woman in repose, leaned back but warped, her limbs are all twisted, some slick distortion of the truth, and it's my favorite because it looks as fucked up as you feel. You don't take a picture, and you never find out the artist's name. I feel someone's eyes on my back and move quickly along.

*(27 likes.)*

*October 3, 2021. Snapchat story.* (& I'd tell you more about the picture but it doesn't exist anymore and I don't remember what we were doing in it except that we were smiling like liars and yes how tragic? but also how safe?

plus holy fuck time is weird & how fleeting some memories are. How permanent we make others.)

"What do you mean, she made you eat cottage cheese for lunch too?" My sister is staring at me, her bug-eyes bugged out even more, and I am in the driver's seat, taking us to an amusement park in a nearby city. We're just over halfway there, and she is on the passenger side—has been commenting on my fast turns and sharp lane switches—but is now staring at me with her huge, light eyes that everyone says they wish they had, that I say I would gladly trade for my almost-black, almond shaped ones, but that she sometimes hates.

When I don't say anything, she asks me again. "She made you eat cottage cheese, too?" I'm thrown off by her *too*, and it's not often that I have no words, but I had made the comment in passing, a warm-up joke about how mom not being around would at least mean less cottage cheese dinners, because I was attempting to cut through the tension that is Our Mother, and I hadn't expected anything but a half-hearted laugh, maybe one genuine chuckle, and so I have no words to hold out to my sister when she asks this. My sister's *too* makes my stomach do a rollercoaster lurch more than anything.

I look in her wide eyes. "What do *you* mean—*too*?" & I feel curds of cottage cheese in my throat & I hear my stomach in the middle of the night, and then later in third period, as I press my hand down hard, like the kind of pressure I could exert is enough to silence a scream.

"I mean," she says, "mom did the exact same thing to me." And then, we're both silent, more normal for my sister than for me. But I have nothing to say, we both have nothing to say, until minutes later, minutes moving more like hours, because now, right now in this very moment, we are realizing something about our mother that we never knew before. We are learning something about each other that we never knew before.

I speak first—I ask her quietly, "Did she tell you to throw up too?" And I know those words were the wrong ones to give my sister, I know I messed up as soon as I ask the question, because my sister's eyes are now so wide, so bugged, that I think they might pop out of her skull, detach from the retina, fall to my floorboard, and rattle into the empty cans that I've never bothered to pick up.

"She didn't."

"She—" I stop. A song I hate is playing on the radio. The truck in front of me revs its engine. The sun has long passed its peak, and I shield my eyes from the harsh light. "What does this mean?"

"It means our mother is fucked."

"I'm confused." My sister nods. Then asks: *will you tell me what she did?*

And so, I tell her. Tell her how *mother put rice cakes in my lunch box* when gymnastics and growing up made my thighs muscular and much bigger than they used to be. How *mother told me I could sweeten cottage cheese with low-fat syrup and berries* when high school started and I ran every day, and practices ran late, and I'd get home after dark, starving, and head straight for our father's desserts. *Mother always said I needed to be careful,* so that I wouldn't end up wearing size six jeans, *and she'd pull yours out of the drawer,* saying that the weight gain can happen so, so fast. *And mother even told me once,* after I had binged for the first time, and made myself throw up for the first time too, and told her I was scared and only did it because I felt out of control, *that making yourself throw up was normal. And that she used to do it too. And that I shouldn't worry about doing it. And that maybe I should do it, if it made me feel better. If it made me feel like I was in control.*

"God, I wish I would've known."

"It's okay."

"I thought she only did that kind of stuff to me."

"I thought the same." I take my eyes off the road for a second. "I thought you were, *are,* so perfect." I look over at my sister, at her huge cow eyes. A memory flashes into my brain—my sister, years earlier, moo-ing at a group of cows we were passing, both of us in the backseat of mother's car. "I'm sorry. I really thought the same."

"I'm sorry I didn't know."

The sun stays in my eyes as I stare ahead. I pretend to be suddenly absorbed by the nonexistent traffic. I turn the radio up until the volume is so loud it hurts. Quietly, I say: "I'm sorry I didn't know, too."

*(You can't like a photo that doesn't exist.)*

*June 3, 2023. Text message from B. "The shitty new algorithm just showed me this photo of yours." (Image attached.)*

I cup my hands together under the sink and watch a drunk couple make out in an open stall behind me. The floor is covered in piss, and there's no soap in the dispenser. The Paper Tiger is a chewed-up spitball mess. At least they're both pretty. They have the blondest, curliest hair I've ever seen. Tongues sloppy. But the music is terrible. I mime forced gagging— stick my index finger in the shallow part of my throat and pretend to retch. Someone walks in and yells at them, *get a room!* I look at my face in the mirror. One-half of the couple yells back, *take a photo it'll last longer!* And I choke on it. So fucking loud.

*(149 likes.)*

# My Father's Spine

They cut muscle from the bone. They tear away the flesh. They remove parts of the body that are broken and no longer alive. Skin is stretched. Skin is pulled apart. Organs are moved around. Sometimes, they never return to where they once were. They reach into the body. And they cut and tear and strip and burn the muscle, the flesh, the bone, the nerve, before putting it all back together again. The muscle remembers. The bone remembers. The body does too.

The spine remembers most of all. The spine remembers the nights when the neck fell asleep funny, the days when the back carried too much weight, the weeks when bones inside the body became slowly crushed, compressed, compacted, broken. My father's spine had nights like that, underwater, sleeping in a small submarine bed. My father's spine had days like that, standing too tall in a place where there wasn't any room to stand. My father's spine had weeks, months, years like that, slowly crushed, slowly broken in an underwater place that liked to break everything. My father's spine, cut and changed and made more broken before becoming more fixed, remembers it all.

My sister is in medical school, so she told me how it would go. The first cut would be on the back, over one of the vertebrae. Black marker sketched onto flesh might guide the surgeon's hands, but it might not. The muscle and fat would need to be moved away, torn apart from bone and ligament, sinew and nerve. Cold metal clamps would split the back in two. And the bone would be white, under red blood and orange fat. A scalpel would remove the lamina, a kind of organic tissue. Then parts of the spine would be removed, milk bone taken from the body.

Our father would be placed in a bowl, a basin, a bag all sealed up. Outside of the body, our father was only medical waste. Outside of the body, the spine was only collagen and compacted mineral. Our father's stolen spine was only bone, already changing into dust. Those bones would be taken away, and gloved hands would replace stolen father with cold metal and stranger-hip. The gloved hands would screw in rods where calcified, shattered disk used to be. The gloved hands would soak up the blood and sew up the muscle and stitch up the skin.

Hours later, the needles would be taken out, the anesthesiologist's timecard would be punched, and the penny-sized holes wouldn't close up for days. Hours later, the father-pieces would be long gone, crammed into red-plastic sealed shut bags, and incinerated. Alongside a grandmother's liver tumor and a child's severed leg, the father-pieces would be made into ash. The bone would become dust much too soon. And on a windy day in the middle of March, cars on I-35 would smell burning plastic, pieces of our father melting in blue flame.

Once the gloved hands stitched up our father's back, the body would begin to heal. The blood would clot, and the nerves would kiss. His skin would slowly rejoin, puckered and mad. But there would always be a scar. My sister told me it would fade, but it would never go away. I tried to picture it, in those terms, bloody and red and raw, as my sister spoke. I couldn't.

When I was younger, I used to go through my father's

closet. I don't know what I expected to find then, but I do know what was always there. His old Navy uniforms, hanging straight, sullen in their neat rows. The white one he wore to marry our mother, next to the faded blues. Medals stitched onto the fabric. Patches of color I had no meanings for.

I used to ask what they meant. But he would never really answer.

"Where I've been," he'd say. "What I've done. Who I used to be."

I'd nod, not really knowing what that meant either. Sometimes I'd pause or walk away. I had to be content with nothing, content with his frown.

But sometimes I'd try again.

"Where *have* you been?" I'd ask. "What have you done? Who did you used to be?"

"It's not important," he'd say. And then, if I hadn't already run off in the way children do, "I'll tell you when you're older."

✕

Before they took him to the operating room, before they wheeled his bed away, there was no joy in his face. The thin gown he wore barely covered his shoulders as he rested on his stomach. The black marker drawn along his spine bled through its seams. The gown was closed with white string, and he said goodbye to us like he used to. He said goodbye to us like he was about to go underwater for months, instead of under anesthesia for hours.

For a second, we were back in early morning airports and liminal color. He stood tall and straight, and his curled, dark hair was cut down to the skin. Our mother still smiled then—our mother wasn't drunk and angry then—and we still held onto her legs and onto her skirts. For a second, we were back in easy childhoods, before any hard falls. He said goodbye like he meant it. He said goodbye like it was something we had to hold onto—hold onto tight—before saying it back or before letting it go.

There are things in hospitals that I've never heard or tasted or smelled anywhere else. Strange noises in a room full of strange people. You have never seen them before, and you will never see them again. Antiseptic and cold coffee and stale food. Unwrapped and half-sipped and never thrown away. Magazine pages flipped from a few chairs over. The pages are from years ago, and they are never really read. Automatic sliding doors, and yells from outside. Automatic sliding doors, now shut, and those yells now from the halls. Everything is white or beige or gray or pale yellow. Everything is sterile and stinking of soap and sad people and death. When the yells begin and the automatic sliding doors open, close, my sister stops talking. It isn't our father's yells, our father's spine then, but she stops talking all the same.

My sister stops talking, and I stop listening. We stare at nothing. We stare at plastic wall and sterilized window. We stare at each other, unsmiling sisters with twin frowns. We stare at the grainy television, playing reruns of some shitty show. Until the automatic doors open again, and the yelling fades and then completely stops, we stare at nothing. We stare at wall.

I think of hospitals. I think of submarines. I think of strange noises in a strange place, full of strange people. I think that submarines and hospitals must be sort of the same. I think that my father must be feeling sort of the same now, just as he did then. I tell my sister this. I ask her if she thinks these things too. She says that she tries not to think of it at all.

The same day, after surgery, we leave. Our father is half-asleep, high on pain medication, and a nurse helps him to the car, giving us instructions on how to take care of him for the few days he'd need help after. My sister is driving, and talking again, about x-ray photographs and spine memories and submarine hollows. And I am daydreaming on the ride back to our childhood home. Red brick and grass now dead, we wouldn't hear yells. We wouldn't taste cherry licorice, medicine thick and hot. We wouldn't smell cold coffee and orange-scented floors, not anymore.

X

I walked through the front door, and nobody was there. Outside, it was spring, muted pinks and orange sky. But inside, the windows were closed, and it was easy to see that my mother had been gone a long time. Cobwebs floated down around high ceiling corners. My father couldn't reach them. Stained glasses sat untouched and unclean. Our father could barely walk.

Outside, my sister helped our father walk slowly—I could see them through back door slats—and I tried not to imagine metal inside of the body. I tried not to picture how the bone was taken from the flesh. I tried to forget shattered vertebrae and the harsh lines on an x-ray page. The images my sister talked of were bloody and red and haunting. The images my sister talked of were orange-scented and stank of automatic sliding doors and ugly yellow walls.

I tried not to think of my father going under—

underwater then, under now. And I tried not to think of the spine with all that remembering, with all that memory. Instead, I tried to think of the weeks to come, the weeks where I would work and go to school online from my childhood home, the weeks where my sister would help clean up the cobwebs until our father could reach dusty corners again, the weeks where our father would heal, the weeks where we all might start to heal.

Days later, he walked through the front door. It wasn't raining then, but it could have been. How easy a memory can be changed. How quick it can be gone—how fast it can be made new. He carried grocery bags to the kitchen, and the limp that was there before was almost gone. I could almost imagine that it was never there.

I watched his body stand tall, taller than it used to— his spine changed and unbent. His smile was back then, and I thought about all the cobwebs that would soon be gone. I thought about all the glasses that would soon be washed, changed in their small way too.

"Are you okay?"

It's the only thing anyone could ask. It's the only thing anyone *had* asked for weeks, months.

"I'm fine."

My sister didn't look convinced.

"Are you sure?" I don't think I was either.

"I'll tell you when you're older."

Years ago, I asked him what it was like under the ocean. I asked him what it was like when he lived with only a few others aboard a submarine. I asked him what happened, down where it was dark and blue. I asked him what they spoke of, down where it was only cold and blank. I asked him what he felt when he first went down. I asked what he felt when he first came up. I asked him why he ever left, why he decided to never go back, why he decided to stay and go and allow his body to break easy like a child's, even though it would never heal like it might have when he actually was one.

I asked him these things as a child. Sometimes, my older sister listened. Sometimes, our mother listened too. Back then, I thought they knew everything—more than me, more than anyone. They never asked all the questions I did. They never asked anything.

But, they did listen. And now, looking back, I remember how they would lean in, move closer, hold their breaths, and wait for my father's slow reply.

Now, I ask him if I am older. I ask him if I am old *enough*. He has a thousand stories. A million rememberings. He has a body that breaks much too easily, a spine that remembers it all. I ask if I am older, and he says that I am. My sister asks if he wants to remember, if he wants to go back. She says my questions and his stories can wait if he doesn't.

But he says that he does. He says that doctors have taken pieces of him away. He says that he wants to answer all of my questions, give us all of his stories, before they take away any more.

*You know you're breathing. You're breathing air. You're feeling air go into your lungs, go out. You know you're breathing. You breathe in, then breathe out. But the moment you go down, the moment everyone and everything goes under, it feels like you've taken a big breath, a huge breath, and it sits there. You take a huge breath, and*

*it sits there, trapped in your lungs.*

*You're underwater for thirty days, sixty days, ninety days and it's hard to exhale. You've been underwater for ninety days, and you know you're breathing. You know you've been breathing this whole time. You know because you're the person who makes sure everyone can breathe. You know because you're the one who makes sure everything works. You're the one who makes sure everyone can exhale. But still, it feels like you've taken a big breath, a huge breath, and you're holding it until you come back up, come back up from all that dark and all that blue. It feels like the pressure might make you explode.*

*You don't think about the sun until days after you've first gone under. You think light bulbs are fine. You think blue light and artificial stars will be okay. You think and think and think—it's your job to think, it's your job to solve problems—but after you're under, after you've been under for weeks, you miss the sun. But suns aren't there. When you're that low, when you go underwater like that, when you go so deep where only inhuman eyes can see, the sun doesn't reach you. There are only lightbulbs.*

*You don't think about the night sky until you first come up too. Down below, there are too many men and too many fake suns and not enough space for it all. Underwater, you know it's breakfast time when the cook gives you pancakes on your plate. You only know the stars are out when you're eating leftovers from lunch. When you first come up, all those breaths, all the pressure, all the time spent underwater in a strange place, in a strange world, collapses. And there are too many stars in the sky when before there was only dull metal ceiling holding out tons of ocean water and death.*

I tell him that humans aren't meant to hold a breath for so long. I tell him that humans aren't meant to be in the dark for so long. I tell him that humans aren't meant to look at dull ceiling when stars are in the sky. And I tell him that he didn't talk about missing me or my sister or our mother, not once.

I tell him that I think hospitals and submarines are sort of the same. I tell him that he went under again, and I tell him that we were scared. I tell him that he's not in a submarine underwater anymore and he's not in charge of making sure everyone can breathe anymore but he *is* still making everything work and we're still here and we still need him to come back up, we still need him to help us make everything work. As I tell him these things, I am a young girl again. As I tell him these things, my sister and I are back in the airport—we are the same, except there is no mother to say everything will be okay. There is only our father, constant as always.

He doesn't answer for a long time. I have not asked any questions. He stretches out his legs. He flexes his feet. He rolls his neck to one side, then the other. He massages his back, and his hands press into father-spine and stranger-hip. His hands press into healing scar tissue. And I think that bodies heal so easily. I think of all the other stuff, all the stuff that is so much harder to stitch up, and cover with a bandage.

I have not asked any questions, but he speaks.

*You don't think about that kind of stuff at all. Once you go down, you don't think about what you're leaving behind if you never come back up.*

*You don't think about your daughters, four and nine, waving goodbye. You don't think about your wife, leaving her all alone, leaving your best friend. You don't think about making sure everything works at home because you have to think about making sure everything works hundreds of feet down.*

*You signed up for this. You signed up for this when you were young and you may not like it all the time and you may have some regrets but you have always done the things you signed up for and you will do this too. You will do this, and you will try not to think of your wife, your daughters, four and nine. You will do this, and you will think of stars instead.*

Our father stops speaking. Our father, constant as always. I ask him if suns are easier to miss. My sister leans in. We are children. He says yes.

# Ashes to Ashes

I am six and singing—we all fall down.

Or I am thirteen and telling my sister that I want to be cremated when I die, *you know, just in case.*

Or I am twenty and cross-faded not because I like it but because someone offered, flicking gray embers to the ground and watching them settle over grass.

I am old, dead already, and my loved ones say goodbye to my powdered, made-up face.

Or I am ash.

Or I am not old, but still dead, and my body sits in a coffin, already burning at 2100 degrees.

Or I am the bone that would not burn and had to be crushed with a heavy mallet instead.

Or I am darkness, seeing only urn wall.

Or I am after: in a palm, scattered.

Or I am six years old, and singing, and then falling down.

Sometimes when I'm wasted, I wonder who will hold me for the last time.

# Some Body

I wake up in a bed wearing nothing but my underwear. I don't know whose bed it is. My phone had been in my skirt, but I don't know where that went either. In the corner of the room, a small TV is on, throwing red light against the dark walls. The end of a horror movie is muted. I look away after a young girl smashes a rock against a baby bird's head. I pull the covers up to my chin. Away from the screen— beige walls, and photographs are taped up everywhere. *Peter Pan,* I think. He smiles in every picture. This is what I remember.

His smile is nice enough, all toothy and wide, but the more I look, the more the eyes terrify me. *Am I remembering wrong?* crosses my mind more than once, more than twice if I'm being honest. And his eyes—those fucking horrible eyes—aren't oceans, dim stars, at all. More like shallow pools, empty as new houses. Next to all the pictures, there's a clock. It blinks, and *3:32* becomes *3:33*.

On the other side of the room is a window. On the other side of the window is a balcony. On the balcony, a boy, no a man, *twenty-two, right at the edge of twenty-three,* is smoking a cigarette. Filter against chapped lips, he blows grey smoke out into the dark air. Clouds swirl around his mouth, caress his face, and he turns to the glass, looks at me. I wave at him—*hello, where the fuck is my skirt?*—but he doesn't wave back.

He's not wearing his costume anymore, and I can't see his eyes very well from the bed—his bed, I guess—but I hope they're kinder than the eyes on the wall. My body shakes. I look at the black sky, beautiful boy. I need to see his eyes. *His eyes are oceans. His oceans are eyes. Hello?* I mouth.

*Why do I feel so strange?* I wave at him again.

From behind the glass, his lips part like he's about to speak. His lips move, but I don't hear a thing. His words are lost. I have just as much trouble finding them as I do trying to find all the constellations in the sky. Orion and Cassiopeia. Sirius and Ophiuchus. All the kings with their shooting arrows. All those lions and ladles. *I can't hear you,* I say, cupping my hands around my mouth, as if that might help, as if he would listen. I sit up, and the sheets fall away.

He doesn't open his mouth again. Just stares. Maybe it's the come down. And I try to see if his eyes really are so frightening, but I am in the way. My reflection. Some girl. Somebody. Some body. I mouth language again, *hello?*

My brain knocks on my skull. *Let me out.* Or maybe it has been pounding this whole time. *Am I remembering wrong?* I ask myself once, more than twice.

I begin to panic. I begin to think I must be dreaming. I convince myself I am dreaming. The room is cold and the navy duvet is stiff and the girl twists the bird's neck *for good measure* and I can't tell if there's blood or not and my skirt is gone but there are my cat ears sitting on his desk and this is not real and this is not me and I thought he was moving in next semester, is that right? No—I am a bird. I whip back around to face him. All I see is my reflection.

Dark hair. Center part. Wavy but more so tangled. It shrouds the girl's face—her face, my face—and mascara mars even darker eyes. Almost black now, my eyes. What's left of her lipstick is smudged across her lips. Was she wearing lipstick? The color is red. The color, he knows it. Her lips—no, mine—he wants to know them better. *Hello? Can you hear me?* Some girl mouths to the boy, no he is a man remember, outside. *Hello?* And I am the bird on the windowsill, the one watching, the safe one.

He shakes his head, ignoring her. I wave again. She doesn't catch what is said. *Why isn't he waving back to me?* Throwing his hands up like *forget it*, he picks up his habit and takes another deep breath. She takes another deep breath. No—I am the one taking another deep breath.

I lay back down on the stiff covers. I shake my head, try to shake the image of the dead bird, the battered skull, away. I try to breathe, slow and even. She tries to breathe, even and slow. Her hands smooth down the fabric. *You are in a dream.* Her hands skim my bare legs. *You are not in a dream.* My hands touch my bare legs. *How strange,* my brain is quiet at first. *How strange* that you have human legs, you are such a funny bird.

But then *my* nails scratch *my* bare legs, *my* freckled legs, the puckered skin right below *my* knee, the childhood scar that is white but will never go completely away. *How strange that they are bare.* And finally, my brain begins to scream. *Get up! Find your skirt! Find her skirt! You need to leave!*

I look at the pictures hanging on the wall. I look at the boy outside. *YOU NEED TO GET UP! Leave this room! Down the stairs and cross the street and almost there and then safe and sound!* The door leading to the balcony opens. *Please, sweet bird, I want you to be safe and sound.*

I have to tell myself I'm fine. The girl on the bed is okay. *Am I?* The boy's eyes can't be half as mean as they are in the photos—his smile is sickly sweet. Look at that sweet smile. Isn't it sweet? She is safe. I am fine. I smooth my down. The pillow she sleeps on earlier is made of me. Look, she holds onto me. Look, she likes it. Look, she is fine. *Is she really?*

I fidget. The girl stands. The boy slides the door shut, turns the lock 'til it clicks, smiles but doesn't move like I do right now. I feel naked as his windows, bare as a person can be, and I don't remember drinking more than two beers, but my head is killing me like I drank twenty, and I suppose I did take all those sips. My eyes slip backwards. My vision turns black. I don't know what's happening. *YOU NEED TO LEAVE!* But it's like I'm finally seeing the stars out on that balcony, seeing stars behind my eyelids, seeing underneath ocean waves, seeing all those lying lions and broken ladles.

And then I see red. And then I scream. He grabs my arm and pulls me into him. My vision comes back—I come back into the room. I am scared, but I look up, into his eyes. *I TOLD YOU SO!* They are cold and blue and I don't remember oceans ever looking like his eyes do now. I think I might black out again, but he keeps me upright. Is that a mockingbird on the windowsill? I forget if I say this part out loud or what I keep inside myself. His nails dig into my skin. Like crescents? But I thought he was a dead star? and I frown.

"I want to leave." I want to go home. He doesn't let go. The bird on the TV is dead.

I run out of breath. I didn't even realize I was screaming. His hands taste like cheap cologne and boy and my blood. I try to move but he's stronger than I am so I can't. *Why are you stopping? Because I have to go back to my windowsill.* The girl's eyes gape open like a dentist appointment *ahhhhh.*

He smiles down at the girl then. Stretches his mouth so his back molars show. I see his bright red uvula. And his smile *is* nice. Look! At! That! Smile! He must be nice, so nice, with a nice smile like that. *But what about his eyes? Look at those eyes!* I stare into them but no—I am the dead bird, and my eyes are very, very closed.

It is the girl who sees his eyes. She is the one who

thinks his eyes are so blue that she could scream again. Empty as new houses, but hey, blue as oceans. It is the girl who should scream again. *YOU NEED TO SCREAM AGAIN!* I hate that I didn't scream again. He moves his hand. Brushes a strand of his hair out of my face. The girl is silently crying. The bird on the TV is dead. The boy is still fucking smiling.

"Hey, it's going to be okay."

# Nerve Ending

*Noun. Anatomy. The termination of a nerve, at the distal end of an axon.*

C plucks guitar strings when I ask him to. Kisses me even when I have chapped lips. His hair curls up but only around his ears. Fingers touch the nape of the neck. Sometimes he sits at his desk and says he can't. No time. Come to sleep, I say. I have a panic attack. Why do you do this every night? I believe that he really wants to know. Play your guitar for me? I hold onto the nights in his parent's backyard when we were both visiting home during the summer. This isn't a guitar, he says. He tells me its proper name but I forget right away. Play that song for me again? He sighs but plays it again. I fall asleep. C is a nice and sweet boyfriend. Once, he breaks up with me and the tips of my fingers go numb for hours.

*There are a total of 17,000 touch receptors and free nerve endings in the palm.*

Z grabs my hand and asks if I want a tarot reading. Her hair is blonde. She cuts it short. We are sitting on her bed which is too soft. I sink in. I feel like I might never be able to move. She tells me her celebrity crush is that actor from School of Rock. Him? I want to know. Him. She wants to know mine so I list ten plus names. Can't pick just one? I think about last night when we met and tell her ten more. Nope, never could. Her ring finger brushes against the thickest vein in my wrist. I take shallow breaths. She taps a message into my skin but I don't know morse code. I let myself sink deeper. There is a not a space of wall in her bedroom left blank. Everything is covered. Even her eyes are covered in glitter eyeshadow. I feel bare. Some glitter has fallen onto her chin. I pray it falls onto me. So? Tarot reading? I say yes then she lets go.

*Nerve endings are the millions of points on the surface of your body and inside it which send messages to your brain—*

J takes my sweater off. Tugs hard on the sleeves when the wool collar gets stuck around my head. I ask if I can put mascara on his lashes because I want to. He says yes then gets mad. Are we just friends? What are you talking about? I like you. I like you too. So? We have our first fight, if you can call it that. Here. His thin lips are turned down and he says my question reminded him of someone else who hurt him. Take my hand. Where are we going? My closet is cramped and I haven't done laundry in a month because my meds have me all messed up and this isn't a closet. It's a time machine, I say. I push him in. I shut the door. I tell him to close his eyes and I close mine too and I spin the both of us around. His back is sticky with sweat. The muscles in his shoulders—leftovers from hockey. Residual, he shrugs. I think I make a whirring noise. This is why I like you, he says this months later, right before he says goodbye, too. He asks if I want to talk about it. I poke his left dimple. About how hot it is in here? It's too warm. We're both sticky. I throw my sweater in the wash. Plus what's there to talk about?

*—when you feel sensations such as heat, cold, and pain.*

I can't do anything about pain, so I focus on the thermostat. I will make my apartment true neutral, even if it kills me, I vow. No goosebumps. Not one line of sweat. One night the power goes out. Electricity burns hottest blue then is gone. I'm burnt out and the cold burns a hole through me this night and fuck I can't even obsess over fixing it. I bundle up in blankets and wake up too hot. I take a cold shower but that makes me shiver. I step out, soap clinging to me, like the bitter taste in the back of your mouth. I hear the soft hum of the AC and rub my hands together warming them up like I like the feel of friction don't like the feel of everything else.

# My Kidneys Suck

I pee into a cup, and my pee is red.

"Fuck." I say it quietly, so the nurses outside don't hear. I hear their movement, the tearing of hospital bedsheets, their loud whispers, on the other side of the heavy metal door separating the bathroom I'm currently in and the temporary room they wheeled me into after I had a breakdown in front of the ER receptionist.

"I feel bad. Her veins are slippery. Hard to catch," says the nurse who stabbed me six times without finding a vein.

I dig my thumbs into my lower back hard, silencing muscle, and I try to stop the sharp gasps that woke me up a few hours ago when it wasn't eight in the morning but three o'clock right on the dot, the hour for witching and kidney pain and maybe all varieties of death by stoning, really.

"It happens," says the other nurse, the nurse who slipped a butterfly-sized needle into my right arm first try.

They don't believe me—this is the problem—and I know they're waiting for the scans I had to beg them to take before putting the good stuff into my IV, but I know this feeling like most people know their lover in the dark. I tell this to everyone when I first walk in, but they think *dramatic! much?* and then ask if I'm on my period, and also have I tried Midol? "No, it's kidney stones," I tell the nurse, I tell the radiologist, I tell the doctor, I try to convince strangers that something is wrong with my body.

"Still, I feel bad. Look at all this blood."

I hear more paper rustling, the stuffing of stained paper and my liquid, me, into a waste bin. "Fair warning," she had given me. "I'm new, but that's okay right?" Paper crunches loudly. "Sure no problem," I had shrugged.

"Before shift's over, I'll find some thicker ones for you," the older nurse says. They stop talking, and I imagine their gloved hands methodically stripping the hard cot of bloody paper. Like a chant. Make it new. Make it clean. Make her new. Make her clean. Sometimes I wonder if Band-Aids are more for other people than for the person with the hole in their arm.

I look down at my hands, pale and nervous, and I fumble with the plastic lid. It takes me several minutes to screw the top back on the cup filled with my red pee. I shake it up and down. My lower back twinges again. I wash my hands, watch stinking antiseptic soap circle in the drain. I say, "Fuck," again. I shake the pee cup until my bloody urine foams up, all bubbles and air pockets, at the top. It's a pretty color, that foam, and I can't even blame the thought on the morphine and IV drugs and whatever else they haven't but will eventually pump into my bloodstream after finding a thick-enough vein. *Hard to catch.* I stare, transfixed, at the lazy pink suds.

"You doing okay in there?" New Nurse knocks hard, and I almost drop their *specimen* onto the floor.

"Is red pee *okay?*" I don't ask. "Doing great—be out in a sec," I say instead. I shake the cup once more for good measure—I want them to find it foaming like that—before setting it down on a sterile, metal tray.

*I pee blood now,* I think. I text my mom, *are you almost here?* I text my dad back, *fuck!*

On the hard cot again. Back in the room that's too close to the nurse's station. And everything is the same except for the new paper bedsheets I've purposefully torn, and the liquid drugs now dripping slow into a fat vein. I might be imagining the thickening of my arm. The bloated, puffy skin I can't stop pinching. I can't be one hundred percent sure, but I swear I'm turning blue.

I'm also on the phone with my sister, but I keep getting distracted, because just out of view, a few feet back from the curtain I wish they would swish close, nurses at the nurse's station talk loudly. And smack sugar-free heart-healthy gum or whatever.

Sam is short, thirty-something maybe, and telling Ben Not Short for Benjamin, about some kid who came in earlier with a severed thumb. "Clean cut, so they reattached it, no problem."

"No problem?" Ben asks. "Kid was four, playing with what, a knife?"

"That's what I wanted to know. And where was the mother?" Sam mimics Ben's tone. One of them clucks their tongue. I think they both sound like chickens. A new voice chimes in, I don't catch the name, but it's full of agreement, full of that stupid clucking too.

"Why are you being so quiet, weirdo?" my sister asks.

"What did they put in this thing?" I flick the clear tube disappearing under my skin.

"In what thing? In your IV?"

I nod.

My sister waits.

"Sorry, yes, in the IV thing—what's in it?"

"For you? Right now? Different pain medications." I imagine my sister ticking them off in her brain. "Morphine, meperidine, fentanyl, hydromorphone, oxycodone, oxymorphone, tramadol. It really just depends." I must be laughing because she stops talking and asks me, "What's so funny?"

"A four-year-old cut his thumb off."

"And this fact is…funny to you?" I imagine her concerned face. "Oh, by the way, are mom and dad there yet?"

"Almost—I think."

It's almost dark outside when the urologist walks into my room and closes the curtain behind him. "Where are your parents?" he asks, as if I'm not nineteen and an adult. When I tell him they're not here yet, he sighs. Looks around the room as if they might be two inches tall and I'm a liar. He sits on the stool New Nurse pulled up next to my bedside earlier so we could play BS on her break, and he's tall with great posture as he scoots further away from me, and his posture might even be too great, because right now he looks like an alien in a human skin suit.

When he says I need surgery as soon as possible, he doesn't look at me but down at his clipboard. And he doesn't laugh, he has a natural frown that deepens, when I make a joke about period cramps and back pain and being dramatic and all the things they tried to tell me when I first walked in hours ago, loud and right. He stays unsmiling, and I feel weird for making a joke, for saying anything at all. I ask him what the scans showed. What I really want to ask is if everyone else is sorry and wrong.

Keeping his eyes on my chart, he explains how the kidney stones I have this time—*I get them all the time*, I scream into a void—are bigger than normal. This, apparently, means I need them—him—to shove something up my ureter and break them up. Fish them out. *Slippery? Or just hard to catch?* He will place a stent in my body to open it all up, but that too will eventually need to be fished out with all the rest. "How long will I be open, *vulnerable?* like that?"

"Two weeks, give or take," he says. There's no emotion there. "And you'll be awake then." He answers the question in my throat. "But it doesn't hurt—not too bad." Quick nod. "Do you understand all of that?" He takes his time asking. Each syllable is drawn out, slow.

"Yes," I say without pause. "I told you—I've had kidney stones before."

"Yes, yes." You recognize this kind of dismissive tone. "So you've said."

I'm pissed off, so I say this too: "My kidneys suck. Do *you* understand that?"

He looks up, and I'm shocked by his green eyes—*too pretty for him*—but he looks down just as fast. He asks if I've been stressed recently—*more than normal* is the phrase he uses—and I tell him yes. His eyebrows go up, as if I should have lied, as if I shouldn't have said anything, as if he isn't staring at my medical history when he should be looking at me. On his clipboard, he jots something down.

"You take Effexor for panic disorder?" he asks, even though he's a doctor and knows.

"Yes. Gabapentin too."

"And would you say you've been dealing with your panic attacks—with, he places his finger over something in my chart, your anxiety and suicidal ideation—*more than normal?*" He refuses to look at my eyes.

"I've been dealing with a lot of *shit*." He flinches when I cuss.

Clicks and unclicks his pen. "Well, that's *something*," he says. "I'm curious—" He is definitely an alien from Saturn. "—I'm curious if you are aware that stress can actually cause kidney stones?" Nope, he's from Mars.

"Yes."

"Well maybe that's something we should work on

then, hmm?"

I say nothing. He clicks his pen, and I seriously consider jamming it through his esophagus. I want to see how aliens bleed. He tucks it away in his coat pocket. Does his Adam's apple quiver or do I fantasize his slow gulp?

His voice is cheerful when he stands to go. "Okay then! See you in surgery!"

I am taken to a different room, up a floor, and handed a flimsy cotton gown. My face is hot as I fumble with the strings in the back—I tie a bow best I can. Looking into the mirror above the sink, I splash water on my face. I press the back of my hand against my forehead, my cheek, the quickening pulse just under the skin on my neck. I am red and I am flushed and I am tangled, matted hair. I am sore, aching vein. I turn around and see my exposed shoulders. My skin shines red and sweaty in the mirror. My neon blue underwear shows through the cheap fabric dress. I'm angry at this single transparency. I untie my bow, yank the strings into a tight knot instead.

They—the nurses pressing down on my syringe, as my heart races quick, as my veins swell up with *the good stuff*—tell me I won't feel a thing. They—my parents, as I stare longingly at the veggie burger I can't eat until after—tell me it's the same thing as falling asleep. They—my sister, as I call her for the third time, asking her to explain the surgery in disgusting detail—tells me how it will go in her clinical way, as if I don't know about the gloved hands that will move my unconscious limbs onto the operating table. As if I don't know about this operating table at all, cold and hard, unyielding, over which my lifeless body will lay. As if I don't know about the vessels, the blood, the organs, my fucked-up organ, the cells in my body that will be manipulated by stranger-hands, touched by unsmiling stranger-doctors.

They all tell me stents don't hurt that bad—they lie—and they tell me I'll be good as new in a few days, a few weeks tops, as though the scans don't show seven more kidney stones scratching against organ tissue. As if this small surgery will scrub all the other fucked-up shit away. As if this surgery will rid me of everything. As if any of this will make me new. As if I am a roll of thin paper that New Nurse can simply tear away and replace.

Two hours later, and I wake up in a bed wearing nothing but my underwear, this feeble hospital gown. I don't know whose bed it is until I look at my right arm, riddled with needle-sized holes, and feel the deep pain below my waist, around the tender flesh where his hands were. I cannot stop myself from gasping—it is too familiar.

I look around and there are no photographs taped up to the wall and my head is groggy but not from date-rape drugs and there is a clock but a safe analog one that I can barely read without my glasses and someone is walking through the door but it is only my mother. Holding a burger out in front of her chest as though cooked soy can bite, and my father, with his warm, brown eyes.

# Nude

As paint, you begin as equal parts red, yellow, and blue. Add white. More yellow. Maybe red, Burnt Umber. Raw Sienna and Goethite as flesh. You look to Botticelli's Venus. Better yet, a cast of Praxiteles'. Collier's Lady Godiva is bleeding onto her horse. And Picasso's 1902 is more Phthalo Blue but see how the spine curves? Yellow Ochre is your shadow. As the polaroid forgotten on an ex-lover's desk, is your knee kept close, pulled inward, like hers too? You are 2.4 inches tall by 1.8 inches wide, thick-bordered and always-bare. Is this what Saint Valentine— from Latin *Valentinus*, from *valeō*, from *strong*—wanted when he wanted love? Flimsy, in his hands. Naked as a glass soda bottle without its label. As the blank space of wall above your old couch. As a body in the tub after some long morning. You watch it fill. Watch it rise. Spill over its porcelain edges. At least Klimt had water serpents. You are only primary colors, reds and yellows and blues now streaming thick across the tiled floor, and you are running out of soap.

# Slip of the Tongue

In an offhand, roundabout, not-my-story-to-tell sort of way, my mother tells me that her mother once sat in an electric chair. I am young, at an age much too young to hear about death by electrocution, and I am confused, because my mother's mother is still very much alive. I lean in closer anyway. When I'm this young, I'm always wanting to know more.

In my head, I see medieval torture devices. Hand straps. Head gear. I don't know what agency means, but the pictures in my brain evoke a lack of it, as men in lab coats fill a not quite sterile room. And I see the woman, my grandmother, my Nana. I help her bake in her small kitchen. Our feet are bare, and our hands are sticky as we eat raw batter. We know we're not supposed to. We laugh. "Why would anyone ever want to put Nana in an electric chair?" My mother grins, has manic eyes, and says nothing more. I see a wooden seat, Nana's eyes—rolled back, like peppermints—and I have no way to tell what is real.

I realize later that my mother confuses electric chair with electroconvulsive therapy. I am older when I realize this, and I feel betrayed for believing a mistake for so long, and I am angry with my mother, all of the time, for this and for the rest. I start raising my voice when we speak, mother and daughter, those once sacred conversations turned sour, and I don't have words for it then but I hate the way she slips up even now, and I hate the way I slip up too.

Once, I say winter elbow instead of cold shoulder. I tell a friend I want to be an eavesdropping flea on a wall, and they correct my mistake with a snort. Telling this story? Piece of pie. It's not, and a tapeworm song has been stuck in my head all afternoon. My mother reminds me of the ways we mess up. My mother reminds me of the ways I'm like her. My mother reminds me of what it means to be a woman who is not perfect.

Every time she said the wrong word, I corrected her and smiled and relished the feeling of having the correct answer when she didn't. Every time she wore a low-cut top, I cringed and asked her if she was *really going to go out looking like that*. Every time she darkened her lids, I fought the urge to throw water at her face, scrub all of it away, cleanse her skin like I thought it needed to be cleansed. She would look at me like I was wounding her, and it made me feel guilty, made me feel like the kind of person who picks pretty flowers out of the ground only to watch them die in a vase on the dining room table, but I couldn't stop myself. It became an obsession. I became some kid's faulty science class paper mâché volcano.

Men leered at her, and I had to stop their looks. Men's wives would look her up and down, and I desperately needed her to disappear into the wall. *Why can't you just stop?* I asked her once. *Why can't you just be normal?* She gave me a blank stare and cocked her head at a 45-degree angle. *Why can't you be a different kind of flower?* She acted like she didn't know what I meant. *You're smarter than this!* I yelled at her, and she refused to cry because it would ruin her mascara. I demanded an answer, and held my hands out, palms facing upward, like how you collect faucet water to splash over your face, and I got mad when she had none for me.

Maybe I'm most angry at the way my mother wielded her femininity like a malleable weapon. When she thought she needed to be meek, she cowered and spoke softly and leaned into mistakes like a big-eyed cow leans into a barbed wire fence, leans into the man who built the fence, leans into the man who is planning to cook the cow for lunch.

Maybe I'm most angry at the way my mother chose which slip-ups to show and which ones to hide. Sometimes, she barely spoke at all, wore lipstick two shades lighter than her preferred color, and carried a cotton swab so the thick eyeliner gathering in clumps around her tear ducts could be removed before anyone might notice.

Maybe I'm most angry at the way my mother could chameleon herself into a room. When certain men were around, she made lewd jokes, and her voice carried wherever she wanted it to. Other times, she recited passages from Psalms, and made me memorize them as well, and prayed for her sins to be washed away, and then prayed they wouldn't carry over to her daughters.

Maybe I'm most angry at my mother because I do understand her.

I mean don't.

But maybe I do.

# Scar Tissue

It is Tuesday. Or at least I think it's Tuesday. I haven't slept in days, and it's dark outside, rain cutting through the last of the heat and sameness of summer, right at the edge of autumn, and I only have a small light on in my bedroom, casting shadows and stories on the wall, in places where it is otherwise naked and bare.

I look in a mirror, the full-length one in the corner, and there are dark circles under my eyes. Purple and palest blue, like day-old bruises, making shadows on my face just like the rivulets of light / nonlight on my walls. I am twenty-three here, now, and yellow bulb makes my cheeks sharp when they are round, my brows dull and tame when they truthfully are unplucked and thick and wild. My face is blue even though my apartment, outside, the rain, my skin, are warm. And I look as though I've seen an old memory, a ghost of a memory, a ghost itself, or, better yet, as though I am one.

I trace the outline of a pink scar, almost white now, under my right kneecap. I am tired but can't sleep. I trace the constellations of scars, red and white crosshatching, some barely there, some newly stitched up, on my arms. I am coming down from uppers but have lost all my numb. I press my fingers against my neck, swallow, feel my hyoid bone jutting out where it should not be jutting out, and I can almost see the inflamed skin in the back of my throat, the flesh that becomes bruised after binging and purging. I am circles and triangles and squares in all the wrong places, an unfinished Picasso painting, a face melting and made of wax, a mosaic of tiles that don't match up just right. I look in the mirror, and I am grotesque—I see scars that are not on my body, but that I feel all the same. I am molded clay that has been smashed with a hammer. I look in the mirror, and I look fine.

I'm alone in my apartment, and the blinds are drawn shut, and I pull my sweater over my head because my skin is getting hot, and no one is looking now, but if I were to open my windows, huge windows touching both floor and ceiling, then my more voyeuristically inclined neighbors would be able to see inside. Foreheads and noses pressed against glass, all fogged up from their warm breaths, they could see the black silhouette of my body, the outline of my jaw bones, the twist of my neck.

Through the rain, through night's cover, I wonder if they might be able to see further, see anything else besides a body that could belong to anyone. I wonder if they might see my eyes, stark against the whites, my long hair, hands running through it, and then over freckled skin, fading now, as I finger my bad dreams. I wonder what they would see. I wonder what I could make them see.

It is past five in the morning, barely, and I'm running with a friend. I am seventeen here, and the path we run on every day before school, made of gravel and rock, is hard underneath my old tennis shoes. One of my socks has a hole right up top, and my big toe sticks out, and sweat is pooling there now. I'm on mile four, with four miles to go, and so I try to ignore it. Instead, I try to think about the sky, dark but getting lighter, spotted with cotton-candy clouds. Or my friend, blonde and pony-tailed and too smart for her own good, a grade ahead of me, and running behind me now. The dog barking a few blocks away, the middle-aged man revving up a push lawnmower is down the road even further. I don't wear headphones, or listen to music, when I run. I like to hear outside.

I hear it all now. I hear the steady hum of driving cars on close roads as the neighborhood begins to wake up. And there's the toll of that one church bell that rings every hour, on the hour, even when it's not Sunday. There is the morning, on mile six. There are the overgrown trees, green and bright and imposing and rude, on the next. There is the path. There are my feet. And there is so much sweat pooling around my big toe, and my toenail is a bit too long, and I think I can feel the fabric stretching, ripping, ruining. I'm running, we are running, surrounded by the overgrowth that could be hiding anything, that we have joked about hiding a serial killer, a monster with seven eyes, a monster with only two, and I trip over the feet I can't stop thinking about. I hit the ground, catching myself with my knees and elbows, before my chin and face can become broken and bloody.

*Fuck.* "Fuck! Are you okay?" She comes running from behind, her blonde ponytail loose.

I pull myself up, wincing from the sting. "Yeah, I'll be fine," I say. "I wasn't paying attention, and the—"

"Here." She reaches around and grabs my elbow. "Let me see."

She's close now, maybe too close, and her eyes are the color of grass. She's tall, much taller than me, and her smile is nice and crooked, her voice even nicer—almost singsong, how she talks, how she speaks as though she knows everything will be okay, even if it won't. She's bent over, now looking at the cut on my knee, and I feel my skin turning cold, clammy, as the blood rushes out.

"You might need stitches." She runs her thumb over the already-bruising skin. "There's a pretty deep cut—

here." Her hand lingers over this new wound, and it's right on top of an old, faded scar that has healed easily since childhood.

"I'm okay, really."

"Well, let's get you cleaned up anyway. I think I might have gauze or something, back at my car."

She doesn't, but she drives me home, music softly humming as I press my hands hard against my leg and try to keep the blood from staining her passenger seat.

"The car's old. It's fine," she tells me. But I feel bad still, and I keep my hands where they are.

We drive without saying anything else, but silence comes easy with her. The car smells like cherry soda and her, and my stomach feels fizzy too. She pulls into my driveway before I'm ready to get out, and I wish I lived further away. She says she'll see me at school, later, and I hear the music, turned up loud, blaring then, as she backs out of the drive and rounds a corner too fast. I wave goodbye. Her smile is a lovely kind of crooked. My knee is still bleeding, and I walk inside, and I eat breakfast with my sister, and I don't get stitches, even though she tells me I should.

*I trace the outline of a pink scar, almost white now, under my right kneecap.* I am laying on the bathroom floor of my apartment, and I cannot breathe. I am nineteen here, and I am texting my boyfriend who lives forty-five minutes away. I tell him about this panic attack, how it comes unbidden, wraps itself around my chest. I tell him it is cloying and saccharine and stifling. I send this text: I think I'm dying. I think I'm having a heart attack. I think my lungs are at capacity, about to pop. I think my ribcage is nearly ready to break.

He texts back and says that *everything is fine. But it's not,* I say. I forget if I send a picture of what I do, or just tell him about it.

After, he calls me. *What the fuck did you do!*

*You can't—*

*Why would you—*

*I don't get why—*

*But you're—*

*But you're—fine.*

My arm is still bleeding when I tell him that *I really don't think I am.*

✕

*I trace the constellations of scars, red and white crosshatching, some barely there, some newly stitched up, on my arms.* I pull the sleeves of my oversized sweater down, and I am twenty-one here, on holiday break, up near Dallas, spending the night with my family at my grandmother's house, and trying not to faint because of the overdose—the accompanying serotonin syndrome—that happened a few days earlier.

It is morning, too early for me, and too early for my sister, and so instead of sitting in the living room with everyone else—cousins, aunts, uncles are here too—we sip warmed cinnamon milk over the dining table, over our catch-up conversation. It has always been easy for us to slip back into old jokes, our habits, and her smile warms me up like my mug. As we rub sleep from our eyes, I almost forget about everything that has happened, almost forget about everything that has sucked, until her eyes go wide.

She grabs my arm and yanks my sleeve up. "What are those?"

"Nothing." I try to pull away. "Don't." But she doesn't let go. "Whit, seriously." Her grip doesn't loosen.

"Call me." She is tracing my wrists, tracing my panic attacks that I'm unsure how to stop any other way. "If you need to."

The conversation ends when our father walks into the dining room, rubs the tops of our heads, and messes up our sleep hair even more. Behind him is our mother, eyes bright like of course they are, and I tug my sleeve down further as she breezes past.

"What are you guys talking about?" She is already dressed, not in pajamas like everyone else.

"*We*," my sister says, "are just trying to wake up."

"Ah. Well." Our mother takes a sip of her cold coffee, leaves a dark lipstick semicircle on the white ceramic. "It's close to ten, so I'd sure hope so."

And our mother smiles, content until she is not—content until later, content until everyone is around the dinner table eating turkey and I am eating my second slice of lemon chess pie and she is telling me to *slow down, take it easy, do I maybe want to go on a run with her later?*

"You know—you're in college now," she says softly, in-between comedically tiny bites of sweet potato, "and it can be hard to keep it all off."

I only nod, mouth full, and she beams, standing suddenly, and I don't know what else to do so I hand her my plate. She's more than happy to take it into the kitchen for me, calling out *we'll go in an hour hon!* and I hear the rest of my pie plop into the sink. She flicks on the garbage disposal, and I wish I was the thing gurgling into nothing.

Excusing myself from the table, I say *an hour sounds great mom!* and I duck into the bathroom and I say *I can't wait!* and I stick my hand down my throat. I make my fingers touch my uvula, and I force the pie I just ate for dinner, and everything else, to come back up for dessert.

*I press my fingers against my neck, swallow, feel my hyoid bone jutting out where it should not be jutting out, and I can almost see the inflamed skin in the back of my throat, the flesh that becomes bruised after binging and purging.* I brush my teeth—I am twenty-three here, again—and I spit into the sink.

I look in the mirror, the small one in the bathroom now, and there are still dark circles under my eyes. There are still scars not on this body but that I feel all the same. I look in the mirror—and I *look* fine—but mirrors don't show everything. I look in the mirror—and I *look* fine— this body *looks* fine—don't we all look like we're doing just fucking fine?—but mirrors don't show shit, really.

# Punnett Square

*Am I evil?* typed into the search bar.

*Spit it out baby,* some lover said.

*When Bhanu Kapil asked who was responsible for the suffering of your mother?* I felt ice in my pancreas.

*Wait do you know the play where all the people turn into rhinoceroses?* I wanted to know.

Well it's hard to say because it's hard to answer plus no one ever stops to ask why I'm doubled over in the 7/11 when I think about it and it's no fun hyperventilating by yourself now is it? Staring at the dirty grout, I choose now to wonder: does a *passing down* even work like that? Suppose if I knew, that would mean I'd also have to know whether her eyes are more green or more brown and everyone knows some things are better left outside of remembering, y'know? I *will* say this: I relish the ringing I don't answer because it means my aging mother hears nothing but her own blisters on the other end.

Oh you don't know? Oh that's too bad. Ionesco? The absurd? I told you about it night before last? Fuck you don't remember? Come *on*! It was right after I explained how mispronunciation kindles realism more than any mirror but no? Nothing there? Well I can show you a review online but don't get mad at me if the cursor blinks too slow because then later I'll stare at my face in a warped spoon like I used to when I thought I was possessed by a demon because my mother spoke of the rapture so often but what? No? I didn't say anything you're tripping. You're hearing things man.

Honestly I would rather talk about your blood type. Or your mother's maiden name because you keep telling me but I forget to listen. Or who you fucked before me. Or who you want to fuck after me. Or why some SSRIs cause brain zaps but others don't do shit. Or if the fire alarm in my old apartment is still beeping because what if it is but what if no one lives there anymore so nobody can punch it silent with the wrong end of the broom like I would? Or about the violent revolution you'd like to incite. I see your eyes lighting up now so *you* tell *me*: what is the circumference of your worst memory?

Okay fine! fine so I want to punch more than goose down and broken fire alarms you happy now? And I wish I could hold the bird whose feathers my head rests on, stroke her sober, that make you grin? I'll throw this in too because who's truly listening anyway: I *relish* my mother's call because my refusal to answer means she hears nothing but her wilting breath, and the memory of harsh silence after my feet stopped kicking her belly 25 years ago, as she doesn't cry into the receiver but wants to. And fuck. Next time you want to hear how my pain bends, just touch the cricks in my neck instead.

# In Case of Emergency, Break Glass

## STEP 1: PUNCH

Water runs red down the porcelain sink, taking my skin, and glass shards so small my father has to pluck the rest out with tweezers, down the drain, through the pipes, and out to oceans or wherever sink pipes go.

*Does this hurt?* my father asks, as he takes a sliver of glass—what was bedroom mirror seconds ago—out of my palm flesh. *It's fine,* I tell him, *but we need to hurry.* We should have left twenty minutes ago, should be arriving at my high school right now, and I should be in the mandated black slacks and a starched, white button-down shirt, instead of the blood-splattered t-shirt I have on now.

*I'm going as fast as I can* he says, and I say *I know,* and I can't be angry with my father in this moment because this is all my fault, if anyone's keeping a running tally, because I am the one who reacts to my mother's snide comments about my shirt not fitting quite right. I am the one who is class valedictorian and should be smarter than this. I am the one who should've been at the school, preparing to kick off senior serve night, half an hour ago now. I am the one who used to bite tongue until I tasted metal. I am the one who decided she was sick of holding back, her, tongue, like that.

But still, I wish he would go faster, yank the jagged pieces out fast instead of the slow, steady way he's plucking them from the skin. As my mother's eyes well up with tears, tears I know are as fake as the alligator boots on her feet, I am also the one fighting the urge to smile. I am also the one fighting the urge to cry along with her.

*There, all done.* My hand is still bleeding, but the sink water is running pink now instead of red, and I touch my hand with the other and feel no glass. *Hurry and change and I'll drive you.* Before I turn, my father adds, *You need to apologize to your mother.* Because I'm a teenager, I'm obligated to roll my eyes. *Do I have to?*

When I was younger, I wasn't the kind of kid to toss salt over my shoulder or fear for my mother's bones. My best friend would be jumping from sidewalk square to sidewalk square, chanting that old chant you know, taking special care to land dead center in each. The boys on the playground would dare one another to cross under the ladder the maintenance man left propped against the school building, and they'd do it, but they'd run back under, the other way, right after. And so many mothers would joke with me and their daughters, chuckling, telling us to make sure we didn't break any mirrors before we slathered makeup on our greasy faces.

*I don't want to apologize.*

But *my* soles would come down squarely on the concrete cracks. I'd walk under ladders and not cross under again. I would on-purpose punch a mirror and scream and think about how good it would feel after, when my mother's face crumpled into nothing, like a dying anthill, almost like mine. *Your parents' backs aren't going to break,* I'd tell my best friend with the crooked bangs and matching socks. *Walking under ladders isn't unlucky,* I'd shout at those stupid boys. *Seven years of bad luck? Silly,* I'd say, under my breath, as friends' mothers left the room, thinking themselves clever and bright.

*I don't even want to look at her.*

And I like to believe that I don't believe in super-stitions now, but you won't see me punching any more mirrors either. Maybe my frontal lobe is closer to being developed. Or maybe, just maybe, my seven years of bad luck *are* almost over—and nobody's been counting—but I've only got one more bad luck year to go.

*Okay but what if I do it later?*

And fuck, I can't stop thinking about how my father's back really did break.

*Okay fine I'll go apologize now.*

## STEP 2: FALL

A strange girl I met only hours ago is older than me, but she is drawing now like a child. Permanent marker on notebook paper, she draws a stick figure with hair, a man, the man we met earlier in the night, the man who screamed at me, the man she screamed at after, in Brooklyn's cold streets.

I never thought I might be here, in her apartment, in this bed. Up until twelve hours ago, I had no idea I would even be in New York City—my flaky friend asked too quickly, and too quickly I said yes—but the sky was the perfect gray, gray and slipping like winter sleep, even though it is summer now, when I found her in the loud, lonely, expensive, cheap, ugly, lovely bar. And she smiled at me like I was a long-lost lover, or something equally as poetic, even though she'd never met me before in her life.

She draws now like a child and then runs to her kitchen, laughing louder than anyone has ever laughed before, and then she runs back into her bedroom, jumps onto her four-poster canopy bed, and her midnight hair sprawls across my lap, gets everywhere. I am one hundred percent either wasted or in love.

In a city where there are so many sidewalk cracks,

ladders to topple over, she is the kind of person jumping on top, walking under without a care, like I once did. When she runs back into her room, she's carrying a large kitchen knife. Slashes it through the air, dangerously close to my chin, and screams *en garde*. She tapes her drawing of the man up on the wall. She is using the cheap, clear kind of tape, the kind that breaks so easily, and she is laughing even louder. I worry about her apartment neighbors for just a second. She looks at me, right as she plunges the knife into the face she has drawn, and she keeps stabbing at her wall for what seems like hours, and even when the knife falls out of her hands she keeps punching at the wall, and her fists are turning red now, and now purple like I feel, and I have no idea what to say.

After, we stare at the large hole she has made. Straight through to the drywall, and the pink insulation looks like cotton candy, falling onto the floor like that. It smells sour and her fat black bunny is hopping around the room, chewing the pink insulation up and leaving wads of it, wet and sticky, behind.

And she is dancing now, the girl, not the bunny, and grabbing the handle and pushing the knife deeper still into the man's lopsided eyes. The hole in her wall becomes bigger. She does not care. I have stopped crying. I want to stop everything. She rushes in, as if she were waiting for this. She grabs my face with her cold hands, as if she knew this was going to happen.

My breath comes out quick, quicker, quickest. I am sitting in the very last row of an overcrowded airplane, middle seat made of rough nylon and plastic, and there is a thirty-something man already snoring, even before the plane takes off, to my left. His head drops down on my shoulder—the window seat is lost on him—and on the other side of me sits his wife. Their very young child sits on her, and the child is screaming. Too young and too confused and too awake for overcrowded airplanes and scratching fabric seat covers and cheapest plastic on barest skin.

The father's glasses fall into my lap, and I hold onto his wire frames, and I try to keep my shoulders level so that he does not wake. Neither of the child's parents offer to switch seats with me. In fact, both looked much too happy when a girl with just a backpack to shove underneath the seat came to claim the one in-between theirs. A sigh of relief. Not mine, of course. And now the child cries and the flight attendant offers the mother a sympathetic look, and the flight attendants keep offering me extra packets of cookies, before turning away, flitting to those help-button lights as fireflies turn to patio fire.

My phone is not set to airplane mode, even though a faceless voice told me to, and I feel panicky, so I text the strange girl I met at the bar last night. I say *thanks for letting me crash on your bed* and *thanks for letting me meet your black bunny named Wednesday,* Wednesday for Wednesday Addams, and *thanks for yelling at the man who yelled at me first,* as I threw up thirty-dollar cocktails on Brooklyn's sidewalk cracks.

I breathe in quick, quicker, quickest, and my phone buzzes, and I see that the girl from last night has already texted back, but a flight attendant stops me from checking it. Doesn't say a thing about the child crying. Doesn't say a thing about the strange man snoring on my skin, barest skin instead of his paid-for cheap plastic. Doesn't say a thing about the child's mother, who looks so tired of talking to children I wish I had something to say to her myself. The flight attendant tells me to switch my phone off and I know she's only doing her job so I listen but I start punching mirrors in my mind because the child is still crying and because the man's beard scratches my shoulder and because I can do nothing else.

Plus this plane is cold, colder than I remember planes being. The screaming child's father stays asleep on my shoulder until the plane lands. The whole time, I hold onto his glasses tight. See my grimace in his lens.

And now this strange girl rushes in, as if she were waiting for this. And now she grabs my face with her cold hands, as if she knew this was going to happen. And now she says it fast—her words stumbling into one another, slurred with alcohol and the night, falling, like our bodies will fall together later. And her *you's* and *me's* and *I's* become like her building, like the red bricks slapped together that make it up. And she says it fast, gets the words out fast, as if all those bricks might start falling down, as if all those words might turn back into red earth and clay, as if we—we who lay on her bed and wait for the brink of night to come and wait for the brink of night to pass and wait to fall from her sixth-story apartment window and wait for her words to stop bleeding together and wait for her words to stop—as if we might turn back into nothing, might become nothing, if she doesn't.

*You, of course, are a rose. But you were always a rose.* I look down at my sad mascara tears that have fallen onto her clean sheets, and as she speaks, as she gets the words out so fast that I can do nothing but stop and listen and fall in love with a memory, we both remember the man who yelled. He screams as if he knows a thing about either of us, as if he knows a thing about being a girl, as if he knows a thing about being a woman, as if he knows a thing about having a body.

*The rose is a rose. And was always a rose. But now the theory goes. Thattheappleisarose. AndthepearisandsoistheplumIsuppose.* This is how her words sound. This is how I remember her words after. This is how her words tumble out, threaten to fall down, promise to build me up, and settle into my memory like bricks.

## STEP 3: SHATTER

Right before the moment of impact, my brain screams that scissors are needed right this second because my brain wants to sever my brainstem in half. Obviously, I listen, assuming my brain knows best, and my hands move for the shears so my brain can migrate down, past my throat ridges, because who am I to judge if my brain wants to live in the dark space inside my thoracic cavity, in-between vertebrae and sternum, where there used to be atrium and the sweetest vena cava you'd ever meet but where now there is only a pinecone. This is where I flake into nothing. This is where everything stabs into me like a fragment.

## STEP 4: GLUE

Water runs red down the porcelain sink, taking my skin down the drain, through the pipes, and out to oceans or wherever sink pipes go. *Does this hurt?* It is not my father who asks the question. It is not the girl who tells me I am a rose. It is not the flight attendant, the overtired father on a flight, the shrugging mother, or the screaming child. *Does this still hurt?* I am the one who asks this time. Another absolute truth? *I don't really know.*

# Acid Trip

**A**bout tonight. The shag carpet is maggots. I scream. Only at first. I scoop up handfuls of them. Stretch out. Across the apartment floor. Is it weird if I tell you I dream about when they'll swallow me for real? He thinks I'm joking. Wants to pull me up. He offers me his hand. I think I sink my teeth into it.

About yesterday. He is melting like strawberry ice cream. Hot cone. Middle of summer. *You look like Neapolitan,* I tell him, two hours after my tongue rolls over the tab, square paper lodged in a back molar until I get it loose and swallow hard. I rub his brown velvet shorts, only half-wishing he was hard underneath. His pink hair drips into my open palm. *What's so funny?* he wants to know. *Everything is so pretty.* This is not how it ends.

About last week. I don't get why you left so angry. I was peaking. You ignored twenty-seven of my calls. *I need you to come back because I can't tell what's real right now.* Granted, my voicemails were unhinged. Did you not like it? You could have told me if you wanted me to stop. But when I told you it was hard to explain, you told me to keep going. Did you not want to know how easy I start to believe everything is a mirage my brain has made up to protect me, how some days I panic and worry that I'm stuck forever in that moment? Listen: I am worried my current life is nothing but a trauma response. You could have held a finger to my lips instead of slamming the door like that.

About last year. I found the box cutter I used on my thighs.

Hope you like West Virginia. Sorry for blaming you for the scars for so long. Sorry for sending you screenshots of my Notes app from that night. I can't get any of it out of my head. Cold air helps some. Other days I don't think about you at all. I remember my sweet black cat crying and crying and lapping up my blood pooling on the bathroom floor. He was so small back then. Sorry if this is too much. Sorry if this isn't enough.

## Breathing Exercise

Start by settling into a ~~comfortable~~ position. As ~~your~~ body settles and ~~your~~ eyes close, bring your awareness to ~~your~~ breathing. Notice the breath coming in, and the breath going ~~out~~. ~~Follow the breath~~ with your awareness...follow the breath all the way in...and follow the breath ~~all the way~~ out...Breathing in, ~~feeling~~ the breath ~~as it passes~~ through your nostrils...~~breathing out, feeling the breath~~ as ~~it leaves your nostrils.~~

~~If~~ thoughts come in...~~as~~ they always do...acknowledge the ~~thoughts,~~ without ~~judgment,~~ and ~~let them~~ go...~~let them~~ drift away like clouds floating across the sky...~~and bring your awareness back to your breath, back to your breathing...back to the present moment.~~

...distracted by a thought about something you have to ~~remember to do perhaps~~...notice the thought, ~~acknowledge~~ the thought, ~~and then~~...~~and bring your awareness back to your breath~~...~~and as it goes out~~...

"Dwelling      in      the      present      moment...
I know this is a wonderful moment..."

...following ~~the breath all the way in~~...~~noticing the~~ slight pause ~~at the~~ turning point ~~as the~~ in-breath ~~becomes the~~ out-~~breath~~...~~the~~ brief pause ~~at the turning~~ point ~~as the~~ out-~~breath becomes~~...

~~Continue for 10-15 minutes~~ *if possible*

...~~aware of~~ your body ~~in the chair~~...opening ~~your eyes whenever~~ you...

Now blink. Did you? You must do exactly as I say. Blink once. Blink twice. Yes of course I'm the same person. Move your toes. Are you? Or are you only thinking about it, more aware of them now? When did you last swallow? Swallow now. What is that thing they—who is they?—say about consciousness? And how does your tongue feel? Thick? Thinner than membrane should ever be? Press it against the roof of your mouth.

Now blink again. I can hear your heart—can you feel it too?—and is your hand on your chest or can you hear the pulse just fine in your throat? Breathe in. Breathe out. What does your wrist say to you? And when did you last think to listen?

Blink. Make sure to count the numbers coming up as fast as you read, not slow like seconds. 1—2—3—you know your numbers but how fast did you read them just now?

Blink! Your aorta fills with blood. The atria contracts, fighting against bone and vessel and always you. Please unclench your jaw. And how do your toes feel? Move them around. Feel free to relax, loosen up. How do you know your lungs are where they should be? What do the holes in your lungs even look like? How do you know? How often do you check? What if they're black because you haven't checked in a while? And what if they're gone? What if you're empty like that? Are you remembering to

blink, dry eyes?

Blink!

Blink!

Not too often. Don't want weird looks.

Blink. Now swallow. Now remember being a kid and not saying *BloodyMaryBloodyMaryBloodyMary* in the bathroom mirror because what if? Remember knocking on wood last week after saying something you really shouldn't have because what if? Remember doing exactly what I say because what if? Good now

breathe in through your nose

1        2        3        4

and out of your mouth

1        2        3        4        5        6

and inhale again

1        2        3        4        5        6

and watch your rib cage

7        8        9        10

expand

11        12        13        14        15

ok quick exhale now again

1      2      3      4

no pace yourself

5      6      7      8

empty yourself

9      10      11      12

release everything

13      14      15      16

slow

17      18

sit with it

19

being uncomfortable

20      21      22

what is unbearable?

23

having no air

24

or too much?

25          26          27

okay

28

closer

29

but first how empty do you feel?

30

or do you feel too much?

31          32          33

yeah same don't you get it by now?

34          35          36

this is the breathing exercise I want you to do

37          38          39

no breathing not yet

40          41          42          43

no you need to feel it

44      45      46      47      48

how being empty feels

49      50      51      52      53      54      55      56
57      58      59      60

before you let it all rush in.

# And If That Mockingbird Don't Sing

*H*ush. My mother brushes my hair like it's hers. It's the same color, dark brown. Until hers turns gray and she dyes it too dark, almost black, because she can't stand the sight of anything ugly. This is what she calls her roots when they grow in. So I laugh and tell her that most hair is dead anyway. But she doesn't like this, and she gets angry at me for suggesting any part of her might not be perfectly, brilliantly alive. *Hush.* Her hands pull at my own roots and I cry out in pain and she shushes before she goes back to slow, calming pulls.

She was always singing. I remember her lullaby. A silencing of sorts, come to think of it now. I used to sing all the time. Can't remember when I did last. My voice sounds too much like hers used to. I don't know what her voice sounds like anymore.

I grew in her body. I cried for the first time in her arms. Her name was the first I spoke. And, when I was younger, it was her hand I went reaching for in the middle of the night. That was the mother I knew then. Now, I have her number blocked, or this is what I say anyway, and the desperate phone calls go straight to spam, as I listen to them once the sun goes to sleep and everyone else in my apartment building is in the REM phase of night.

Her eyes are hazel with spots of light green, and they are lightest in the sun, and they used to be darker, but she says she stared at the sun when she was younger. I don't know if that's true, if that's how dark eyes turn light, and I'm almost scared to check, but that's what she tells me, and so this is what I believe. Sometimes I catch myself staring at the sun, and when I remember how mean her eyes could turn, I look away so quick I feel my neck twinge.

How do I begin to explain my mother? When I try, I feel like I have blue skin, like I am asphyxiating, like there is no air left in the room to breathe, like I am a microwaved lung, all deflated and chewy and tender like that.

My mother occupies space like carbon monoxide fumes. I think I must be trapped inside a single-car garage, no vent. I think I must be running out of time.

I fall asleep. I wake. There is no yellow sun. There is my blue skin, an echo of my childhood bedroom's blue walls. I cry, a sort of song, when she gathers me up in her arms. A scraped knee. A bad day at school. A fight with my older sister. She is always singing. I am always listening.

I fail at writing her, my mother. I think the problem is that there are too many of her, you see. There is the mother I knew, and the mother I don't. There is the woman I'll never know, and the woman I do. I eat nothing except the dust I gather on my finger and pop inside my mouth.

When I was a child, we were close. I must have loved her more than anyone. And I think she loved me so much because I looked like her, because I could have easily grown into a near perfect replica, but I'm less sure of any claims that come out of my childhood memories, the older that I become. And she told me so many stories. She tells me a story now in the yard on the large porch swing, the wooden one we always swung on, and it's one of the first times her eyes turn truly dark.

It's the first night of summer, summer before my eleventh birthday, and my mother asks if she ever told me how her other husband died. I blink stupid. I blink no. It happened a long time ago, she says, happened when he went up north with a few friends. It was supposed to be a hunting trip, a guy's weekend, a few days where they could all shoot the shit, shoot their guns, shoot whatever. She wasn't there when it happened—she tells me this as the sun starts to fall. But she tells the story anyway, as though she was, as I do now.

The day ends like every other day has ended before. Yellow light wrinkles into blue. Songbirds fall silent. Insects swarm to light. And maybe insects swarm to light during the day too—this is an admission my mother makes—but maybe it's easier for us to notice certain presences in the middle of certain absences. I think I raise my hand to ask my mother a question. I think she ignores it. I think she grabs ahold of my fingers with her long, spindly ones, and forces my arm back down.

And all too quick, the moon is visible. Such a tiny sliver of a silver thing. And suddenly the moon's cheese face is full. I ask my mother how both things can be true at once. She shushes me, and then continues her story.

The moon lights up the men's half-circle, an imperfect ellipse, locus of points, lights them up as they gather close in snowy wood. Bearded, grizzled, red in the face as drinking men often are. They are shadows, but shadows that wear orange, the most neon shade there is, and bright reflectors on the sides of their hats, warding off stray bullets and curious beasts and curious men.

Night comes. One of the men suggests they head back to camp. But the other voices are louder, and not good at listening. The men stay in the wood for a while longer. They gather close, closer, the closest men ever get, until they accidentally rub up against another's shoulders, until they bounce away like atoms off the side of a box.

The yellow light wrinkles into blue—and then suddenly everything has. It's dark. Empty, except for the hunters standing out in the cold. Silent, save their stupid drunk words, their boots marking up the fallen snow. Their guns sway, are slung across dropping shoulders, and their hands hold near-empty cups. Amber is passed around until that is gone too. And their breaths come out in wisps, like gray smoke or chimney soot, and they soon forget about deer hooves and rabbit feet and fox fur and tracking any of it.

It's a cold night, but the men sweat in their long underwear and neon vests. It's a cold night, and the wood longs for sleep, but men are not known for letting sleeping things lie. It's a cold night, but guns do not chatter like teeth, and metal does not shiver into something else when the temperature drops below freezing, and the human men can make strange sounds, but guns make stranger, inhuman noise. One man, shorter and grayer and slower than the rest, drops his gun suddenly. As it falls in the snow, it is eerily soundless.

Nobody cares, but everybody laughs. A different man pulls

a second bottle of amber out of his pocket. Well, what's this? Surprise, surprise. Another joke. One too many red-in-the-face grins. Another sip, a slip. And then there is a gunshot. There is *the* gunshot. There is someone's clumsy thumb.

White is marred by red. Pink snow and a body, unnatural and twisted, falls to the ground. The one voice—the man who had suggested going back to camp only a few drinks earlier—retches. Another stumbles to his crumpled friend. Another digs around in pockets, looking for a phone. Finally, *finally*. The forest is quiet. One color wrinkles into another. And finally, *finally*. And everything sleeps.

I am a child, but my mother smiles like one now. I don't think I sleep that night but eventually I crawl in bed with my sister because mother's door is locked and she smells sour anyway, smells like the alcohol she lies about loving later. I ask my sister if I can sleep beside her, *please, just for tonight*, and she says yes so fast, so fast like she knows. She strokes my hair softly, never hard. I ask her if she wants to hear what mother told me in the yard, but she pretends like she doesn't hear my question. Or maybe she truly is asleep. Some things you never get to find out.

My mother changes. I don't know when it happens, but she becomes a mother I don't know, a person who I will never recognize. She is irrational, angry, cutting, guttural, harsh. It's most terrifying how she can yell at me, throw sounds more animal than human my way, and then plaster a smile on her face in the very next second. My mother becomes reminiscent of metal, of a thing that doesn't shiver. Or maybe she does shiver. Maybe her body does homeostasis another way.

Sometimes, I think about all of her stories. I don't know how many of them were true, what true even truly means, or if she believed them herself. In another life, she was doing lines off someone's chest. She was coked out with her first husband's friends. She was sleeping until four in the afternoon, coming down from an acid trip. She was talked into a threesome with a woman she barely knew. I am scared I'm like her, even though everyone reassures me that I'm not. But I do some of those things, I say. But you're not a mother, they always have a comeback. But she wasn't *just* a mother, I point out. And she wasn't a very good one to you, they pat my head like I'm a stupid, stupid doll. I roll these words around on my tongue, maybe my mother was just a woman trying her best, but I never say them out loud. But I don't know if that's quite true either.

Like my mother, I used to sing all the time. Eventually, I stop altogether. Eventually, she stops too. I grow up, and my mother sings no songs and I don't ask her to and when I get scared I reach for a hand that isn't hers. It doesn't take long before I start to hate what makes us the same. I hate my dark brown hair, almost black, too much like hers even now with the box dye. I hate my eyes, how I find myself staring straight into the sun. I am afraid I'm more like her than I'll ever admit. I scare myself most, thinking about how things get passed down. In the end, my solution is simple: throw the moldy bread out entirely. In the end, I just stop singing. No more songs come from her or from me or from anyone in that red brick house. I move out and don't return because I can't. I forget words to songs I used to love. I tell people, *no I haven't heard that one. Sorry, I'm just not that good at remembering names.*

Our mother is rail thin. Not then, but now, later, in the pictures they take of her after, not in the pictures that collect dust and are fading in old family albums. Now, later, after, she is rail thin. And we, me, my sister, do not recognize our own mother as we pass her on the street. We do not see her in line at the grocery store, buying sugar and flour and the brown eggs she always said were better than all the rest. We do not see her at the movies, buying one ticket only, and sitting all the way at the very top, by herself and eating popcorn with extra butter and extra salt and extra cheese. We walk on the sidewalk, and so does she, but we only see a stranger, sad but always smiling, across the busy road.

The yolks are more orange, not yellow, this is what she'd say. This is one of those funny things you remember. The yolks are more orange, she'd say, and this is how you know that certain eggs are better.

It is like this because she has made it like this, we tell ourselves at night. She is the mother who was more like the child. She is the mother who made us, the child, grow up quick and grow up different and grow up when she herself could not. She is the one who did so many *not good* things, the one who let too many *not good* things happen, and she is the one who, at the end of it all, tried to burn the house down. She is the one who tries to burn it all down, burn us all up, burn herself all up, in all that trying.

My childhood bedroom is going to kill me. The memories, I mean—they threaten to. When I go back there, I am blue skin and dust bones and tooth trades and mother lies and brain holes. Like a songbird, these memories mock me.

After my mother does a stint in the psych ward, I forgive her because how can I not? After I write about that memory, I delete it from these pages because not yet. After she cheats on my father, and after she tries to burn the house down, I decide there are certain things that I truly cannot. I give myself permission to mourn my mother for a week before I force myself to move on and pretend like the mother she used to be never existed at all. Still though, I miss how lovely her voice sounded before.

But what of the lullaby? What of the child who was hushed? I want to know the answers to everything. Fuck, I feel like I know nothing at all.

This blue room is really going to kill me. My feet are up against the doorframe. My head is unnaturally bent. The ceiling and the floor and the wall and the other wall are all the same now. My body is tucked into a ball, and I am unsure what is up and what is down and which way the bed used to face. Maybe I am the bouncing atom. This bed and these bed linens and even the dust I suck off my finger are all gone now. There is only this blue room and me. There are all the doors I refuse to open. There is the silence. Do I dare even ask: where is my shiver? There is the mother I don't know calling too much, the mother I knew forgotten like her songs. But I refuse to think about any of it. I fail because I forget that negation is a thing.

It is like this because, in all honesty, we have made it like this too. She lit the match—she was the match, she still is the match—but we knew, or at least, I knew, I know. And we let her become flame anyway. We let the striker burn. Yes, she tried to burn the house down, burn all of us down, burn herself down. But we—I—knew. I know, I was the one she told those stories to. My sister is the one who listened to my snores. And there must be a reason our father always asked if we were okay, still asks us if we are okay today, he finally is starting to seem more okay, today. We knew she was the match, is the match, but we are the ones who let her try to burn it all down, burn us all up, burn herself all up, anyway. We let her burn. We washed ourselves in kerosene then. And we wash ourselves in kerosene still. I wonder what she's singing. I wonder if I ever will again.

My sister's hands still. I mimic her shallow breaths, feigning best I can too. She pretends to be asleep. Or maybe she really is fast asleep. Her bed is easy to sink into. Her lungs rise and fall. Rise and fall. Rise and fall. The steadiest a thing is for me then. In this moment, I think my sister pretends to be asleep. As if she doesn't want to hear mother's songs. As if she isn't a child herself. As though the moon is hardly a sliver. *Hush.* As though the moon's fat cheese face is fuller than it ever will be again.

# Diastema

A space / of separation /
between teeth of different
functions / especially biting teeth
/ & / grinding teeth / but also
everything / else.

Means there is a gap inside of me
that people keep trying to fill.
Also: lucky teeth. Also: what is
the difference between
something being inside of me,
and something being me? I am
better at questions than answers.
This is why I date philosophers.

Plus the worst part is how loud
absence is. It's like tinnitus—or
something equally as distanced,
without, an external source. Let
me put it for you like this: is an
ear worm really screaming if the
only person who can hear its song

is you? Answer: well, it depends on whether you're a reliable narrator or not. & if you believe in absolute truths, or if you believe that pixels are a thing that can be manipulated into something else. & how you define screaming. Don't forget that part.

So I don't know what to tell you, only that I keep refusing to fill myself up with things held out to me like communion wafers, and other people keep looking at me like I'm crazy. Every six months, my dentist frowns at blatant absence, ugly void, my smile, and asks me to.

More than twice, I stand in front of a mirror and try to make absence appear in-between my legs, tucking my stomach in and pushing my lower spine out. Even now, I sit and stare at my

thighs—sweat makes them stick
together—and there is an uneasy
kind of friction present. I'm not
sure whether I should lean into it,
or spread my knees apart like men
do in public chairs. In the end, I
try not to move because the noise
that would follow is an
embarrassment. Plus my mother
is home. Just kidding. But the
walls in this house are thin.

I grow up confused about which
gaps are okay and which ones
need to be eradicated.

I grow up, but I still don't know
how to feel when I realize I used
to eat through my mother's
umbilical cord. At the very least,
this is an irony I can clutch onto,
if not her, if not much of anything
else.

Later, I eat cereal in my bathtub
but the squares become soggy
and the grain unravels like faulty
DNA.

This is why I keep practicing,
looking at absence.

Also: the water in the tub is cold.

One of my art history professors
pulls up Leonardo da Vinci's
Vitruvian Man, and I can't stop
staring, but not at the lines, at the
yellow paper underneath, just
barely peeking through.

Another kind of irony is this: you were once trapped in your mother's uterus. For a long time, you were only small clusters of dividing cells. And, before you became *you*, before you turned into this person, before you were a screaming child in someone else's un/steady arms, you were somebody else, just a *part* of some body else, until you took that first breath outside of your mother's body. Before that, you were cardiac tissue and webbed toes. You were hardening long bone and half formed lung. You were a black and white photograph stuck to the side of the fridge, all blurry and small and—in all honesty— really fucking gross.

To summarize: once you were a space, a gap in the middle, the annoying moment right before the pixels download and become visible, a product of the biting teeth and the grinding teeth and also everything else in your mouth and also something

something negation, plus that one
thing about lack, as the white
nothing on the page, once you
were a space, a gap in someone
else.

& the drawing depicts the ideal
human body (we are told this), a
man superimposed over
himself—and I remember
thinking: *how sad.* How he's stuck
forever like that. In the smack-
dab middle of a jumping jack, in
motion but not, a perfect
mathematical equation, trapped
in a single circle, a single square.
In the back row, I bring my pencil
up to my mouth. Wedge the
eraser in-between my own blank,
as the professor talks about men
and science and art, as two
hundred plus students in the
room pretend to listen then file
out then forget. The only thing I
wonder now is if their bodies
remember sitting over their
notebooks, hands cramping, plus
the shapes they made, that
meaning, the all of it, and the

everything it wasn't / isn't, too. I don't pack my things up five minutes before class is officially over. I sit in the room until the overhead light times out and turns off and I am alone in the dark. & I am mostly content, this is what I am told. & I lie, because I do wonder about more than that, back then, even now.

Here's a sort of truth: I used to wake up early, and let myself fall over, into the pavement, into that particular kind of space, where something can be hot to the touch but also cold. My palms are confused when I bend over and let my blue morning hands burn like on-purpose fires. I don't really run anymore.

& here's another: I have a theory that singularities in black holes are gaping holes of anger. & I think I'm waiting to become one.

Anyway: I would like to
sandpaper my bones.

Also: what happens when the
parts of me that people want to
fix aren't parts at all but absences?
Do you know how it feels to have
someone tell you they don't like a
part of you that isn't even a part
at all?

& this is what they call a lack.

Sometimes, though, the body
keeps what the brain cannot.

Sometimes, though, you grow up and realize that *a lack* is just another thing you'll have to shove in a box and bend over and pick up with your legs! not your back! and move when your lease is up, too.

*Body memory*: because I might as well be a spine with all that fucking remembering.

Because there may / may not be some / thing in-between sinew / nerve / vein / organ / me / & my memories / & this is the gap they want me to reconcile. / ! / ?

And my tongue rests in-between my two front teeth like always. And I think I like the pressure.

And my tongue slides in-between absence. And I choose to let it stay there awhile.

# Bloodletting

Last night, I held a knife in my hands. I did not cut my palm. I did not prick the pad of my thumb like I wanted. Last night, I held a knife in my hands, sharpened earlier for the dinner I did not make, and I pressed the cool side of the blade against my face. I let it rest until I couldn't tell the difference between object / weapon / me. Last night, I dreamt I was a poltergeist kicking bodies and throwing tables. Last night, I dreamt I held my body as though I loved it. Last night, I held a knife up to my carotid and I took a breath and I felt my too-fast pulse and I exhaled suddenly, when I realized how comforting it all was, the closeness of this body I know. I forget what I do with the knife. The bed curves around my spine. This is a strangeness I know. Then red. Then black. Then red. Then black. Then red. Then black.

# Acknowledgements

I am deeply grateful to Ariana D. Den Bleyker—my editor, the founder and publisher of ELJ Editions, and the person whose belief in my work made *These Strange Bodies* a real, tangible, able-to-hold-in-my-hands thing. You are such a light in the literary world.

Thanks are also due to all the wonderful teachers who have enabled me to write honestly and openly. Benjamin Reed—your workshop at Texas State is where I felt as though I finally found my voice as a writer, where I first tried to write one of the most challenging pieces in this collection, "Some Body." And Katie Cortese, the best thesis advisor and professor at Texas Tech—many of these pieces found their way into that first fiction workshop as "autofiction," but after, you made me feel safe enough to finally call *These Strange Bodies* what it was: my real life. Your feedback helped shape this book, and my writing, into what it is today.

I am forever thankful for classmates and friends at Texas Tech who read early drafts of these pieces, especially Marcos Damián León and Nicolas Rivera. I am indebted, too, to other readers whose feedback proved invaluable, especially Paula Cho and Syed Ali Haider.

And thank you to the family I found after moving across the country, fourteen hours away. Mike Speegle, Amelia Skinner Saint, and Bekah Bahn: you are all such lovely writers and even better people—and my sanity is hanging on by a thread because of you.

I am forever thankful for Riah Hopkins, my roommate for the better part of my PhD, and the person who continues to deal with my 4 a.m. freakouts—including the writing of this acknowledgements page. You're like the other older sister I never asked for, but that I adore all the same.

Thank you to the other wonderful people at USD too, especially Lee Ann Roripaugh, whose hybrid poetry workshop led to the creation of more experimental pieces like "Punnett Square." I am a better writer for knowing you.

Annie and Laycee! Thank you for being the best hype men from across the country—I love both of you forever.

My parents are responsible, in part, for me being a writer—thank you forever, for always having books in the house when I was growing up. Dad, thank you for always supporting me so that I can do what I love to do, write and create.

My sister, Whitney, is terrible at answering phone calls—and yet, she somehow knows exactly when I'm calling to ask weird questions about the body. Whit, thank you for always picking up when I truly need you.

And thank you to my favorite reader, Matt—you already know how much I love you.

# About the Author

Court Ludwick is the author of *These Strange Bodies* and the founding editor-in-chief of *Broken Antler Magazine*. Her writing has been nominated for Best of the Net and the Pushcart Prize, and can be found in *EPOCH*, *Denver Quarterly*, *Variant Literature*, *Stonecoast Review*, *Oxford Magazine*, *West Trade Review*, and elsewhere. Court's visual work has shown at the Louise Hopkins Underwood Center for the Arts, and has appeared in publications like *Harpy Hybrid Review* and *body fluids*. She is the recipient of a Sioux Falls Arts Council Artist Grant, and she has taught workshops on hybrid writing and experimental form, most recently for The Dakota Writing Project and Vermillion Literacy Project. Court holds an MA from Texas Tech University and is a current PhD student at the University of South Dakota. She lives in Minneapolis with her lucky black cat, October, where she is currently at work on her second book, a creative-critical project about bones, memory, and mommy issues.